PROFESSIONAL Drinking

A Spirited Guide to Wine, Cocktails, and Confident Business Entertaining

JIM SCHLECKSER

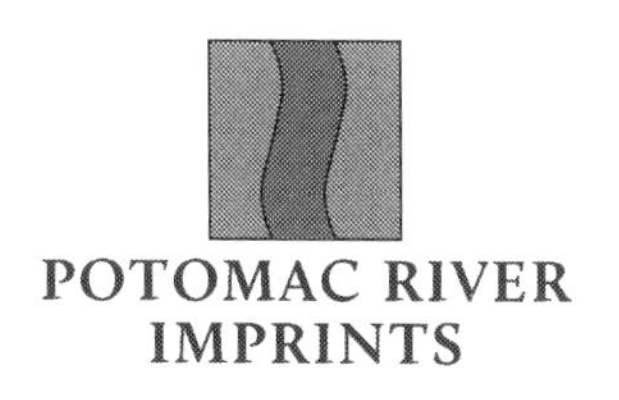

POTOMAC RIVER
IMPRINTS

Published by Potomac River Imprints
P.O. Box 60602
Potomac, MD 20859

Cover design by Sheila Parr
Book design by Alex Head, Draft Lab LLC
Cover image: © Stocksy / Helen Rushbrook
Image credits: wine glass icon, p. 3, p. 20, and chapter 10 images by iStock.com/vectortatu; p. 13 by iStock.com/vectortatu and Harper Head; p. 47 by iStock.com/melazerg; p. 83 by iStock.com/Pan-Pavel; p. 123 by iStock.com/Alhontess, with adaptation by Alex Head; p. 139 by iStock.com/vectortatu, with adaptation by Alex Head; p. 157 by iStock.com/Alhontess, with adaptation by Alex Head; p. 181 by iStock.com/Arkadivna

ISBN: 978-1-7350044-0-2

Printed in the United States of America
20 21 22 23 24 10 9 8 7 6 5 4 3 2 1
First edition

This book is dedicated to my father,
Henry Schlecksер,
who started me on my wine journey and taught me
the value of great company and conversation.

CONTENTS

FOREWORD

AS YOU PROGRESS THROUGH YOUR career, you learn more and more about just how much business is conducted in a bar, in a restaurant, at a networking happy hour, or in another social setting. Okay, it may not be where the contracts are signed, but it is almost always the place where relationships are created, trust is won, and decisions are made.

I wrote *Exactly What to Say* as a primer on how to put people at ease and bring them along a path, using well-chosen words, to a positive outcome for you both. Many of the examples are designed to help readers progress a conversation, gain clarity in decision making, and overcome indecision. What I didn't cover is how to create the context and the environment for an engaging and progressive conversation. Let's face it, if you are comfortable and at ease, you are going to do a better job of listening to what someone has to say. You will also do a better job of being heard and inevitably make more of your conversations count.

Since many critical business conversations happen in social settings and often over an alcoholic drink, the ability to operate confidently and elegantly in any of these environments is critical to the art of persuasion and business. People do believe that skills in one area transfer to another, and if you are to be credible, you can't fumble with the wine list or be awkward with the Sommelier.

Jim Schleckser addresses all this and more in *Professional Drinking*. I know that I learned a bunch of things that I will put into action in my life, both personal and professional. He covers a great variety of information on wines, beers, and spirits without creating a typical boring wine or cocktail book. This basic knowledge of all beverages is sure to give you confidence in any environment. I will say, as a bourbon drinker, that section could have been considerably longer!

Perhaps even more interesting and helpful were the tips on handling yourself in a restaurant, ordering wine, tasting wine, managing the wine service dance with the wait team, and tipping a Sommelier. The section on entertaining at home was equally important given that more and more, we are doing business at home. I have brought people into my home a few times as part of a business process and the results really have been remarkable in terms of the deep relationships that developed. Even if you never intend to use your home in that way, the material is equally relevant for entertaining friends and family.

My career has brought me all over the planet, entertaining and being entertained by all kinds of people. Some of those experiences were remarkable—and not always in a good way! Many have been forgettable. And some were magical, elegant events where the time flowed effortlessly and the end came all too quickly. Incredible relationships that will last for the rest of my career were created. The business became easy. In retrospect, I know now that I was in the hands of a professional drinker—somebody who was confident and elegant and prioritized the goal of enjoying time together and building life-long relationships.

This book is essential reading for all, whether you think you entertain for business or not. Ultimately, the relationships we build and retain are what define us, and this book offers skills and knowledge that help us create, enhance, and maintain powerful relationships.

Phil M Jones
Author of Exactly What to Say

INTRODUCTION

FAR TOO OFTEN, POWERFUL AND intelligent executives are reduced to a quivering mess of jelly when handed the wine list at a fine restaurant. They're completely out of their element and wary of being embarrassed in front of important business partners or even friends and colleagues. Unfortunately, the usual way to learn has been by making mistakes, which is mostly how I did it, or by subtly asking for the advice of a friendly and knowledgeable business associate.

Professional Drinking takes on that challenge by offering a clear understanding of entertaining around wine and spirits, including the basics of booze and how to handle yourself like a pro in a restaurant, at a business event, and at home. If you want to be comfortable in all of these settings—and learn a bunch of great tips, enjoy fun stories, and have a few laughs along the way—this is the book for you.

We will cover the basics of the most popular wine and spirits, the most common questions, and some suggestions from a professional drinker. Then we will head into the restaurant environment, where most business entertaining happens. You'll learn how to handle yourself with the wine list, working with a sommelier, tipping, and a bunch of potentially socially disastrous and embarrassing situations. We then wrap up by entertaining at home, when to do it, and how to do it with elegance.

If you are looking for a comprehensive guide to wine, spirits, and cocktails, this isn't it. I have found that the more a book presents, the less I retain. The good news is that you will be armed with the basics you need to feel confident in almost any business entertaining situation—and hopefully not be too bothered when you don't know something.

Many people take wine too seriously, especially in professional settings. It's designed to loosen people up and to have a good time. To be fun.

There are very few bad wines out there and all wine fits a purpose, even cheap wine. If you're getting the chance to sip wine with friends, any wine, while having a great time, what could be better?

That leads me to my two most basic wine rules:

Rule #1: Like ice cream, sex, and pizza, there is no bad wine.

Rule #2: Wine is fun.

So, grab a glass, find a comfy seat, and let's explore the world of professional drinking together.

PRO TIPS AND STORIES

You will see over 50 of my best tips and stories scattered throughout the book, marked by the wine glass icon. If you don't read anything else in the book and just buzz through the Pro Tips, you'll be a much better and more confident Professional Drinker.

Part One
PROFESSIONAL DRINKING

[1]

WHAT IS PROFESSIONAL DRINKING?

THE TERM "PROFESSIONAL DRINKER" MAY evoke an image of a fraternity brother, with the same phrase on the front of his T-shirt, crushing his 12th beer can of the evening on his forehead. But that isn't what we mean by the term in this book.

If you have been in the presence of a professional drinker, you know it. They order an interesting cocktail and encourage you to give one a try as well, and it's delicious. They'll confidently take the wine list and engage with the sommelier, ultimately ordering well-priced and delicious wine that pairs well with everyone's meal. They know the cadence of the wine service, how to taste the wine, facts about the grapes used for various wines, and maybe even a story about the wine you are all drinking.

Few of us have the kind of background that lets us serve our clients and guests in that manner. There is simply too much to know, and people in the wine and spirits industry revel in their advanced knowledge. They don't make it easy. But it would be great not to sweat when handed the wine list or feel the need to always go back to one wine we know most people like. There are thousands of great options, and exploring them with friends is great fun, but the risk of making a mistake or embarrassing yourself with a bad wine at a business function is formidable.

Ideally, we would all be comfortable entertaining our clients in any setting, from a restaurant to home. It really doesn't mean you have to take on a part-time job studying wine and spirits. A basic set of concepts and rules of thumb will serve you well and increase your confidence around the table.

My intention for this book is that you finish it with exactly that, the confidence and knowledge to be a professional drinker. You should end the book with the basics of most drinks, but it doesn't go into the level of depth of a traditional wine, beer, or cocktail book. Rather, we will drive through most of those topics reasonably quickly and spend a lot of time on how to handle the situations that normally arise when doing business entertainment. You'll have all the knives in the Swiss Army knife of professional drinking, but the nine-blade version, not the 30-blade version! Armed with tools and techniques for almost any situation, you will be a professional drinker, impossible to fluster, and able to show a good time to people you work with and want to impress.

[2]

HOW I BECAME A PROFESSIONAL DRINKER

YOU MIGHT WONDER HOW I became a professional drinker.

I want to be clear: I would not recommend my path to most people. Many of my wine friends have a wonderful knowledge of the space and did not put themselves through this process I am about to describe. The good news for you is that I did, and I will share the most important ideas I learned to help you become a confident professional drinker.

My first experience with wine and spirits happened when I was young. My dad would let me sip sweet cordials after holiday dinners. But what really stands out in my memory was a case of wine, a 1982 Château Haut-Brion, he was gifted by a business associate. This was an incredible first-growth Bordeaux and, at that time, possibly one of the best years in a very long time. He would open a bottle and cook up a nice steak every time I came home from college, and we would indulge. I never knew wine could be like this. It changed my views and interests in this mysterious beverage. W. C. Fields said, "It was my first wife that drove me to drink. I've never written to thank her." In my case, it was my father who started me on my journey with wine and spirits.

I then embarked on a global business career, where I've entertained with fine food and drink in 28 countries. Most recently, I have been running a CEO advisory business that involves dinners with these high-level clients. Those experiences have given me some insight into business entertaining at all price points. It was a wonderful period of discovery, seeing new lands, meeting interesting people, learning different cultures and customs, and, of course, sampling the food and drink of each country. During these many years of business entertaining, I was able to refine my wine palate a bit. But few wines equaled that magical case of the red wine my father had served. Over time, I have shifted to embracing an attitude of gratitude around wine—I just want to enjoy it. I have also yearned to know more.

In time, I fell in with a group of wine lovers, led by my friend Scott Greenberg, the Vine Guy, and I struggled to keep up with their wine smarts. A dozen wine books graced my bookshelves, but I must admit the knowledge never stuck. So, I decided to pursue a certification in wine to increase my knowledge. Like a lot of people, I watched the Netflix movie *Somm*, and I thought the level of mastery demonstrated by the sommeliers was incredibly impressive. After a little bit of research, I signed up for the Introductory Sommelier class and certification at the Four Seasons Hotel in Baltimore—though I only put in a marginal amount of studying.

Being a sommelier is a time-honored position that goes back hundreds or even thousands of years. It requires a ton of knowledge about geography, viniculture, viticulture, wine laws, and service standards, among many other things. The goal of the sommelier is to help the clients at a restaurant engage with the complex topic of wine in an enjoyable way. The standards are controlled by a guild, the Court of Master Sommeliers.

The First Master Sommelier test was given in the UK in 1969, and in 1977 the Court of Master Sommeliers was established as the international testing body for sommeliers. They continue to be the premier arbiter of what a sommelier must know and the level of their knowledge. If someone in the wine service business is serious about advancing his or her career, they will begin to move along the path toward master sommelier, usually ending short of this top certification.

In my case, the introductory class was taught by four master sommeliers, and they led us on a whirlwind tour around the world of wine, including the Deductive Tasting Technique used by sommeliers to blind taste wine—just like in the movie! When I was handed the test, I knew I was in trouble and had vastly underprepared. When they gathered us all up at the end of the day and handed each of us a glass of Champagne, calling the names of those that passed, I was pretty sure I was going home with nothing. But I was hooked and had already started looking at dates for my retest. By some small miracle, I passed. Luckily, they never gave out the actual scores. As my son says to torment me, "Cs get degrees too, Dad!" My certification still hangs on my wall.

From that incredible and challenging experience, I set my sights on becoming a Certified Sommelier, or level 2. To calibrate the hubris I had when setting this goal, there are only around 9,000 Certified Sommeliers in the world. As one moves up the certification process, there are about 1,000 Advanced Sommeliers and about 250 Master Sommeliers. Since the beginning of the space program, which is roughly when sommelier certification started, there have been 550 astronauts. It isn't easy.

The movie *Somm* showed the three parts of the sommelier test: theory, blind tasting, and service. While the introductory test is just a paper test, all the other levels follow this format. While the Master Sommelier test is probably 100 times harder than the Certified test I was to take, the elements are identical.

The first problem with the Certified Sommelier theory content is that there is no book you can study; it is designed like a guild where the more seasoned sommeliers teach the newer ones. Since I was not working in a restaurant, I needed to learn my theory somewhere else. The Capital Wine School is not far from my home and I dug in, taking specialty classes when I could but working my way up another more theoretical program, the Wine and Spirits Education Trust (WSET). Over almost two years, I progressed to their Level 3 or Advanced certification. This involved hundreds of hours, thousands of flashcards, and an entire week of cramming before the final test. Eight nervous weeks after the test, I got my good news and I passed.

Sommeliers need to understand all beverages in the restaurant, not just wine. I studied waters, spirits, cocktails, sake, beer, and other beverages on my own, as my groaning bookshelves can attest.

Blind tasting is used by sommeliers to deeply understand a wine and tie what they see, smell, and taste to their theoretical knowledge. It looks like a parlor trick when we name the grape, country, region, age, and quality without seeing the bottle, but that skill comes from a lot of tasting and studying. I luckily found a weekly tasting group with an advanced sommelier, Ellie Benchimol, who was incredibly generous with her time and knowledge. Every week, she would gather a dozen candidates for Certified Sommelier and taste three white wines and three red wines. Believe me, at 11 in the morning on a Tuesday, I spit my wine after tasting. Together, we tasted hundreds of wines, attempting to discern the wine without seeing the labels. Inevitably, we would miss a few and learn as Ellie told us why we missed calling the wine correctly. By repeating this dozens and dozens of times over a few years, I refined my blind tasting to acceptable levels and could call the wine correctly much of the time. When I correctly named a few of the six wines we tasted, I always left with a bounce in my step.

Service is the last element of the test, and I had fortunately worked in restaurants for more than six years through high school and college, including waiting tables for years. Ellie helped us all prepare for the mock service we would need to pass by peppering us with wine and spirit questions while we served the table.

One fateful day, almost two years to the day after I passed the Level 1 test, I headed to New York to take my Certified Sommelier test at the International Culinary Center. The night before, I crammed flashcards and texted my wine friends and those who provided moral support. The next cold morning, I took a brisk walk to the school to wait with 47 other nervous, caffeinated candidates for the theory and blind tasting segments of the test. We were led into the room to meet the eight master sommeliers proctoring the test, then were given our wines to analyze followed by the 50-question test. Even with all my preparation, I wasn't certain I had passed the blind tasting, but I was comfortable with my theory section. Each candidate is then given a time for their mock service test with a master sommelier. I had hours to kill, so I wandered the streets of Chinatown trying not to think about what was to come, which was impossible.

My service test was toward the end of the day, and I had 15 minutes to do a mock service in a formal dining setting while being asked dozens of questions by one of the rock stars of the wine business. The next table over was one of the master sommeliers from *Somm*, which had inspired this journey. Yes, I was nervous. My service went well, no spilled wine, and I could answer almost all the questions. After thousands of business dinners at great restaurants, I was able to provide refined, unflustered service, even under pressure, which might be the most important part of the test.

At the end of the day, they gathered us together, all 48 candidates who had the same stressful day as me. Standing in a rough circle, holding our Champagne, the leaders said their thanks and began to hand out diplomas. The pile of paper was thin; clearly not everyone would be going home happy. The top scorers came first, followed by people who had passed, including a few people I had become friendly with across the day. While I was thrilled for them, I dreaded the potential of ending the day empty-handed. The 12th diploma came up...Jim Schleckser! I yelped with joy. You are given a pin that represents the new rank with your diploma and we all busily pinned them on each other. The joy ended with the 18th certification being handed out. Out of our class of 48, only 18 passed all three parts of the test for a 37.5% pass rate, a bit below the national average. My train home flew by as I happily messaged friends and family. After two hard years, I had passed.

Advanced Sommelier is not in my future, as it requires multiple years of work in service, in a restaurant. While that was fun in college, I am probably not heading back to that environment, except as a client. One thing I did realize through all that effort is how little I still know about wine and spirits. The field is immense and complex and would take a lifetime to understand even partially. I'll keep learning, but at my own pace and purely for fun.

This brings us back to what a professional drinker might be. It's someone who has some knowledge about wine, spirits, and how to order. They also realize that they'll never know it all and that's okay. They use that confidence to entertain friends, clients, and customers and make them comfortable. The relationships that can be built over a wonderful meal together with some wine can't be replicated. By the end of this book, you'll be a professional drinker—without the two years of studying I went through.

[3]

WHICH GLASS IS MINE?

THE FIRST THING A PROFESSIONAL drinker needs to know is which glass on a table littered with glasses is theirs. This might be the most common mistake and starts the evening off with unneeded stress.

I have worked with hundreds of CEOs and executives over the years in my career as a coach. We've accomplished great things together like building game-changing business models, upending entire markets, and taking companies public.

Yet, in all that time, and among all the suggestions and feedback I have ever handed out, there is one piece of advice that my clients tell me is the best I have ever given. It involves a simple tip to remember which bread plate or water glass is yours when you go out to dinner.

I know: not what you were expecting, right? I can't tell you how surprised I have been by the number of times my clients have come back and told me how useful this piece of advice is.

Now I'll share it with you.

As an executive, you probably eat out often—maybe entertaining clients or even attending charity functions. Picture this: As you sit down in your seat, you're presented with an array of plates, silverware, and glasses. The same goes for your neighbors on either side of you. In fact, the plate you're supposed to use to put your bread on as well as your water glass both seem to be in neutral territory. This is particularly bad in round tables and long banquet tables. Unless your parents sent you to a Miss Manners class as a kid, how the heck are you supposed to know which one is yours?

Here's what you do. Hold both of your hands out in front of you so that both palms face each other and are about six inches apart.

Now, take your index or pointer finger and touch it to your thumb on each hand so that you make two circles. Make sure to stretch out the fingers on both hands as well, kind of like you're making the "OK" sign with each hand.

But what else do you see when you look down at your hands? How about the letter "b" in your left hand and the letter "d" in your right?

Good. Now connect the dots. The "b" stands for bread, which means your bread plate is on your left. The "d" stands for drink, which means your water glass is on your right.

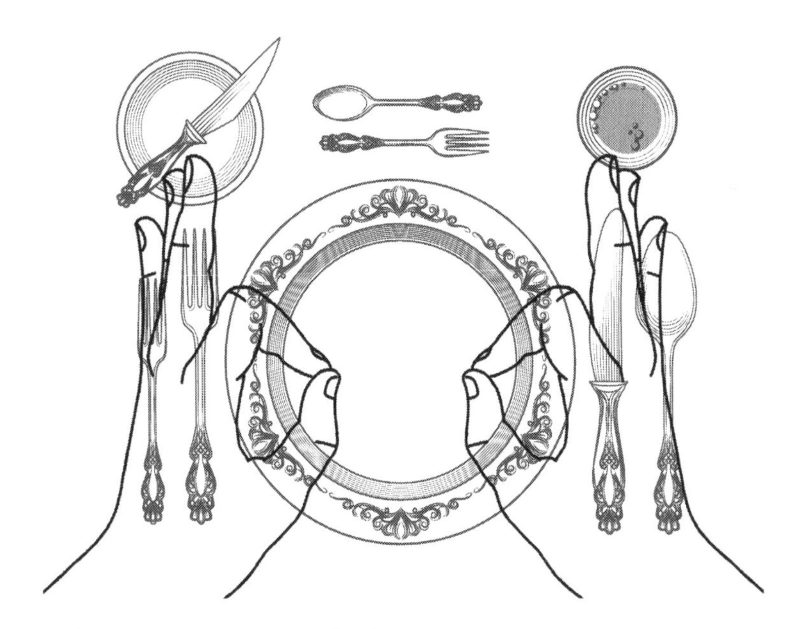

Easy, right? Mystery solved.

It's been very gratifying over the years when I've actually been out to eat with clients and I see them looking at their hands in a "b" and "d" under the table to remember which plate and glass is theirs.

Once you have it down for yourself, don't miss the opportunity to share it with everyone at the table with you. Not only is it a great icebreaker; it's also a chance to share a tip with someone that they will remember for the rest of their lives.

[4]

DON'T GET DRUNK, EVER

WHILE WE'VE ALREADY STATED THAT drinking is fun, there's also another rule to keep in mind: when it comes to drinking professionally, you should never overindulge. It's bad form no matter the occasion, especially at the annual holiday party. Any time you are socializing where you earn your money and where your future is at risk, don't jeopardize it by drinking too much in the hot tub with the entire software development team. One good tip is to plan on arriving a bit late—say 15 to 30 minutes—and then leave early before things get out of control. No good decisions ever get made after 11 p.m., so avoid those bad decisions.

PRO TIP

Stick to one drink an hour to stay sober.

The primary rule of drinking is the equivalency rule:

1 Drink = 1 Beer = 1 Glass of Wine = 1 Shot of Spirits

The math of getting drunk is pretty simple. Consider that a 150-pound person can consume two alcoholic beverages—a glass of wine, a beer, or a shot—and reach the legal limit of technically being drunk or "buzzed." A normal healthy person can metabolize about one drink an hour, depending on body weight. That means that if you have a three-hour dinner meeting over the course of which you consume three to four drinks, you shouldn't be over the legal limit—especially if you've been eating as well. This will vary by person and weight, but it's a good tip to keep in mind.

Timing is also important. You can't hang around for five hours, drain a six-pack, and hit the road and expect to be sober. My preferred approach is to have a few drinks early and then slow down as it gets later in the evening. I'll usually switch to water or another non-alcoholic beverage the last hour or so.

DILUTION SOLUTION

The more water you can consume while you're drinking alcohol, the better. Alcohol is a diuretic and you need to replace the liquids you lose, and beer doesn't count. Water helps flush the headache-inducing aldehydes that form in your brain as you digest the alcohol. One of my rules is to follow every glass of wine I drink with a glass of water. It won't make you less inebriated, but you'll feel a bit better the next morning. For the record, coffee doesn't necessarily make you sober, but it does make you a wide-awake drunk!

If you prefer a mixed drink, go with something that you can mix with ginger ale or another soft drink; just tell them to pour light. The side benefit of ginger is that it reduces nausea.

RIDE-SHARING SERVICES SAVE LIVES

There is no excuse for driving a vehicle under the influence. Period. All stop. If you have crossed the line of consumption or are even close, order a ride. You can get your car tomorrow. Even better, when you plan to have drinks at an event, get a ride-sharing service to the event. That way you don't have to worry about consumption and won't be tempted to hop in your car because you are "just a little buzzed."

If your economics are tight, the designated driver strategy is well accepted and one of your crew can take their turn as the driver. I have a few friends who don't drink for personal or religious reasons and they are great ones to invite since they'll never be tempted to have "just one." Common courtesy is to pay for the night out for the buddy who is the designated driver as a thank you.

[5]

HANGOVERS: AVOIDING AND CURING THEM

IN THE LAST CHAPTER, WE said you should never get drunk at a professional drinking event. But if you do overindulge, there are ways you can mitigate the effect. It happens.

One strategy is to think about "pregaming." Now, I don't mean the kind of pregaming that the college kids do, where they pound a few shots before going out. I mean getting something into your stomach before you start drinking. More food in your stomach means you won't get drunk quite as fast since food can slow the absorption of alcohol. For example, I know Russians who eat a bunch of yogurt before they start hitting the vodka, and it seems to work for them.

PRO TIP

Consider pregaming with vitamin B12.

Alcohol is a diuretic, and along with the water that exits your system, lots of vitamins go down the drain too. The key vitamin to processing alcohol is B12. A lot of doctors I know will pregame with a B complex vitamin and water. They hit the same after drinking and the morning after. Don't worry when your urine turns orange; that's the excess B12 and it means you have plenty on board.

Your other go-to strategy is to drink plenty of water while you're drinking. My goal is always to target one drink per hour followed by a glass of water. That means the waiter or waitress is constantly refilling my water glass. I may have to make a few visits to the restroom, but I am able to flush the aldehydes, or adverse chemicals, that cause hangovers.

When I get home, I'll pound at least a liter of water and pop an Advil. (Warning: Don't take an Advil ahead of time. It can put some stress on your kidneys.) I may have to get up in the middle of the night to go, but I'll greatly reduce my chances of waking up with a headache.

Which alcohol you select can have an effect as well. In the process of making some spirits, the makers want to have elements from the raw material in their final product for color and flavor. Unfortunately, these minor chemical compounds known as congeners can amp up your hangover the next day. Spirits that are high in congeners are whiskey of all types, tequila, and Cognac. Liquors that are low in these hangover-enhancing elements include vodka (the lowest in congeners of the spirits), gin, and rum.

If you do wake up hungover, you have a couple of options beyond continuing to drink water to flush out your system.

- **Drink electrolytes rather than water.** You'll lose a bunch of electrolytes during a night of drinking, so a sports drink or two can be exactly what you need to restore some balance to your body chemistry. I know several wine gurus who use Pedialyte the "day after the night before," and they claim it helps.
- **Caffeine.** It's hard to beat a cup of coffee to get some energy after a late night. I'll admit that there are times coffee doesn't sound like a good idea to my stomach, so I'll drink it with some sugar and cream. It's much more tolerable and gives me the caffeine I seek.
- **Hair of the dog.** A time-honored tradition used by bartenders is to tame a hangover with a little bit of alcohol,

like a Bloody Mary or a mimosa. I can say from experience it does kind of work.

- **Eat some fat and carbs.** If you're hungover, it can really help to eat something—even if it might be the last thing you want to do. One of my favorite breakfasts after a night of drinking is to have some spaghetti with parmesan cheese, lots of cracked pepper, and egg. It's a poor man's carbonara, but I get a nice dose of protein, fat, and carbs, which seems to take the edge off my hangover.
- **Vitamin B Complex.** I mentioned B Complex as a pregame strategy, and it also works the next morning to elevate the critical B12 vitamin to process the alcohol that might still be in your system.
- **Do nothing and binge Netflix.** You've abused your body if you have a hangover, and it would be appropriate to give it a rest. If you can avoid any major commitments, especially ones that involve thinking, you should. Your body deserves a day on the couch plowing through the latest series to drop.

PRO TIP

You're probably not allergic to the sulfates in wine.

A lot of people say they don't like to drink red wine because they get an allergic reaction to sulfates. The truth is that winemakers do use some sulfur in the process of making a bottle of wine to control mold, mildew, oxidation, and pests. But these are extremely low levels we're talking about. There are more sulfates in a piece of dried fruit like an apricot than there is in wine. If you think you're having an allergic reaction to the sulfates in your wine, or your hangover is from sulfates and you can eat dried fruit with no issue, it's probably something else.

Part Two
DRINKING BEFORE DINNER

[6]

BEER BASICS

BEER ISN'T CONSIDERED THE CLASSIEST drink, but I must admit after a round of golf on a warm day, it is hard to beat. You can't go frat party crazy when doing "business golf" or at an event, but many times, I'll have a beer in place of a cocktail. It's a great way to hydrate a little and pace yourself for the evening. I'll usually switch to wine for dinner, but instead of a martini or a Manhattan, a beer is an acceptable approach.

For those of you worried about mixing beer and wine, I always remember the old aphorism, "Beer before wine, you'll feel fine. Wine before beer, you'll feel queer." I always interpret queer as sicker than a dog, but beer first has always worked for me.

Beer has been brewed for thousands of years, back to the Beowulf days of mead. This beverage has lots of variations and modifications, only limited by brewmaster creativity. I am going to hit just the top types of beer you'll run into and want to taste.

The building blocks of beer have been the same for a very long time. There are a few ingredients in all beers:

Malt: There are a few grains that are used for beer making, most commonly wheat and barley. In both cases, the grains are run through a kiln to heat the grain and convert the starches into sugars that are accessible by the yeast for fermentation. This is called malt. The roasting also gives nutty flavors and a darker color.

Hops: With intense aromatics and a bitterness that balances the sweetness of the malt, hops is one of the main flavor elements in beer. It is also a natural preservative.

Yeast: Yeast is a bacterium that loves sugar and converts it into alcohol. The brewmaster might use a naturally occurring yeast in a craft beer or a highly specific commercial yeast for a volume production. Yeast can add fruity notes to the beer.

Water: Beer is mostly water, so brewers need a good source of pure water to make great beer.

Other stuff: German purity laws require beer to just use the elements above. Outside Germany, lots of other elements are added to beer to create the beverage a brewer desires, including honey, spices, and other elements limited only by the imagination.

There are a few other characteristics that define a beer.

Specific gravity: This defines the density of a beer compared to water. Lighter beers are very close to water (insert your favorite joke here), and at the other end, some beers are a meal in themselves, filling your belly to the point of skipping dinner.

Alcohol content: In the brewing process, you can push a beer to very high levels of alcohol or keep it more moderate, appropriate for a weekend picnic. It's worth noting the alcohol content to keep track of your consumption. I once unwittingly consumed two very high alcohol Canadian beers and had a little problem when I went to stand up!

Bitterness: The bitter flavor that is common in many small craft-brewed beers is induced using hops. I am personally not a fan, so I am careful to ask about the bitterness of a beer before I order it. Many people love it and think it makes the beer more interesting and flavorful (which it probably does—this is a me issue).

Carbonation: Not all beers have the same carbonation level, or amount of bubbles from retaining the CO2 during the fermentation process. Simple canned lagers are usually pretty bubbly, and a nice English cask ale will generally be a bit flatter. This one is based on personal preference and how much you like to burp.

Color: The color of beer can run from a very pale straw color (like Coors Light) to deep, dark browns, almost black. The brewmaster manipulates the color through the toast level on the grains used to make the beer. A heavily roasted grain makes a darker (and generally a little sweeter) beer.

Here is a quick summary of the beers you'll want to taste to open your palate a bit.

PRO TIP

Drink lighter beers in summer and heavier ones in winter.

When I do go for a beer, I'll usually mind the season, shifting to lighter brews in the summer and the darker, heavier stuff in the winter. I just prefer the refreshing nature of a lighter beer when it is hot out and the belly-filling and comforting and warming nature of a heavier beer when it is cold out. Of course, in Ireland, Guinness is always on tap!

Pilsner or Lager: This was probably your first beer (hello, Budweiser!). In my case, this was an Olympia beer stolen from the fridge and drunk in a hiding spot in my backyard as a misbehaving youth. Lighter amber in color, and cleaner in flavor, these beers are sometimes divided into Czech and Bavarian style. They are generally quite carbonated and have less bitterness from hops. Most light beers fall in this category, with similar flavors but lower intensity due to the lower sugar level and dilution required to hit the alcohol target. Budweiser and Stella Artois are examples of pilsners.

Dark Lager: Dark lagers are very similar to an amber lager, but the malt is toasted to a higher level, yielding a darker brown color. They are smooth, less bitter, and nicely carbonated. Modelo Negra and Shiner Bock are dark lagers.

English Ale: Usually served at cellar temperature, these ales are fruity and spicy when compared to lagers. They will be darker in color from the toasted malt they use and slightly higher alcohol with limited carbonation. In England, you better order an ale or, as they call them, a pint of bitter because that's what is on tap. I enjoyed pints of Courage and London Pride when I was there.

IPA: IPA stands for India Pale Ale, which is ironic because it was brewed in Britain and sent to India for the expats and the local population. The strong hop content preserved the beer for the long sea voyage and gives it the classic bitter flavor. Lagunitas IPA and Goose Island IPA are two mass-market IPAs (and almost every craft beer is an IPA too).

Wheat Beer: While most German beer is from the lager family, Germans are also famous for their wheat beers. These beers use wheat as the primary grain rather than barley and this gives the beer a wonderful fruity and spicy note. They have an amber color and are generally well carbonated. Blue Moon and Hoegaarden Witbier are perfect examples. If you get to Germany, be sure to try their wheat beers.

Stouts and Porters: Two of the most popular original beer styles, these dark silky beers are a meal in themselves. They were popular on the docks of London to fuel a river porter for a hard day of work (hence the name). The malt is kilned until it is a dark espresso color, which gives wonderful flavor complexity and color. Historically, stouts and porters were aged as well to take the harsh edges off the beer and give them the creamy texture. Guinness is a classic stout and Anchor Steam makes a popular porter. This class of beer is a great one to see the creativity of the beer maker at your local craft brew pub.

This list is hardly comprehensive. There are many variations and permutations to beer, just like wine. But I'd suggest you give each of the above styles a try, although perhaps not in the same sitting. You might find a beer that really speaks to you and is different than your father's Coors Light!

[7]

CHAMPAGNE AS A COCKTAIL AND MORE

CHAMPAGNE. THE WORD ROLLS OFF the tongue and sounds luxurious, just like you are about to celebrate a special occasion. But wine with bubbles is fun anytime, and I'd suggest that we can never drink enough bubbles! It makes a delicious and festive cocktail even when there is nothing special to toast.

THE HISTORY OF CHAMPAGNE

We can thank the Benedictine Monks for creating sparkling wine in 1531. They bottled wine before the fermentation was complete and the excess carbon dioxide stayed in the wine, making it bubbly. An English scientist named Christopher Merret published a paper nearly a century later in which he documented how later adding additional sugar and yeast induces a secondary fermentation in the bottle to produce even more bubbles. This happened right around the time punts were added to the bottom of glass bottles, which allowed them to hold the increased pressure of the gas created.

PRO TIP

Dom Pérignon didn't discover sparkling wine.

While the stories claim the monk Dom Pérignon discovered sparkling wine, he didn't even enter the abbey until six years after Merret published his paper disclosing the now popular Méthode Champenoise.

SPARKLING WINE

Bubbly wine is now made all over the world, but all bubbly wine is not Champagne. That product is grown in the Champagne region of France and uses very specific grapes, usually Pinot Noir, Pinot Meunier, and Chardonnay. The use of the name Champagne has been protected in Europe since 1891 and more broadly in the Treaty of Versailles after World War I.

The names for bubbly wine vary around the world: in Spain it is Cava; in Italy it is Franciacorta or Spumante; in South Africa it is Cap Classique. Germany uses Sekt, and in other parts of France it is called Cremant. But for most of the world, it is simply called sparkling wine.

CHOOSING CHAMPAGNE

The classic method of making Champagne is Méthode Champenoise, now called Méthode Traditionnelle. The process is like that described in Merret's paper. The grapes are harvested and pressed, and the first fermentation process is completed to exhaust the sugar in the grapes. The wine is then bottled and corked with additional yeast and some sugar, which causes a second fermentation, creating carbon dioxide that stays in the bottle in the form of bubbles. The dead yeast cells, called lees, are removed after a period of exposure to the wine through a process of moving the yeast to the neck of the bottle called riddling. These lees are then frozen and removed quickly from the bottle by uncapping it. While it is open and before the cork is inserted, a sweet dosage is added to set the sweetness of the Champagne.

The resulting chalky, high-acid wine is one that is perfect to serve with food. In fact, you can easily go through an entire meal, pairing strictly with Champagne. Most of us stop at a welcoming toast or perhaps through a cold fish course and forget that this bubbly drink can easily pair with pasta and meat entrées and even finish a meal with style.

There are a few types to consider, but I'd recommend getting the best sparkling wine you can swing, as the prices don't go up that much, but the quality does.

Non-Vintage: A lot of the Champagne you will see in your local liquor store is non-vintage. What this means is that the maker has blended grapes from a few different years, thus eliminating the ability to mark it with a particular year. This lets them maintain a house style of Champagne even in years that aren't great by blending wines from prior years. You'll know it is non-vintage since there won't be a year indicated on the bottle.

Vintage: Only in exceptional years will the Champagne growers get together and declare that the wine is good enough to be vintage. The bottle will have a year on it to indicate it is vintage. This means that all the grapes used to produce the wine are only from the year indicated on the bottle.

Tête De Cuvée: This literally means "head of the vat," but it signifies the best of the best from a high-quality producer. These wines are vintage, are usually named as premium, and are produced from the best parcels of premier and grand cru vineyards and only in the very best years. That means your bottle will carry a year indicating when the grapes were grown. It will also have a fancy name like Winston Churchill, Cristal, or Dom Pérignon. Vintages of this quality normally happen perhaps three times a decade as well.

Don't be intimidated by the range of sparkling wines; lots of them are very reasonably priced and are fun to drink. My recommendation is to try a few bottles of sparkling wine from different countries and see what you like. While that special French Prestige Cuvée might be perfect for a college graduation celebration, bubbles are great for everyday drinking too—perhaps celebrating making it through Wednesday. And for the purposes of business drinking, it makes a great cocktail.

[8]

THE LOWDOWN ON LIQUORS

A PROFESSIONAL DRINKER HAS SOME basic knowledge of liquors and spirits, even if they don't regularly imbibe them because their guests might prefer spirits. I am just going to cover seven major liquors, but there are dozens I am not covering including variations of the ones I have here.

Spirits are made from anything that has sugar in it or even starches that can be converted into sugars and fermented. Humans have been very creative in finding things to turn into liquor from their surroundings, and the regional variations come from these different raw materials. Some of the popular raw materials that are fermented include corn, sugarcane, wheat, potatoes, agave, and various fruits.

One of the limitations of a fermentation process is that the yeast can't take very high levels of alcohol. In fact, yeast dies at around 10 to 15 percent alcohol, depending on the strain of yeast. This range is the maximum for wine, which is simply single fermented grape juice.

If distillers want a beverage with a higher alcohol content like a spirit, they must take the output of the fermentation and concentrate it a bit. Distillation is what is typically used. That means the liquid is boiled and the relatively volatile alcohol boils first and goes into a vapor. A cooling coil is used to turn the alcohol vapor into a liquid, which is captured. This is an experiment many of us did in high school chemistry class, except not with alcohol for obvious reasons. Once other items in the mash start to boil, we stop the process, so the alcohol doesn't become contaminated with the non-alcohol elements in the mash. The alcohol captured is pure and usually must be diluted down to the target levels for bottling.

Some spirits are made with a single pot and a single distillation and retain much of the original flavor, but others have multiple stages and lose much of the original nature of the mash.

People will generally talk about spirits in terms of proof, which is simply two times the alcohol by volume (ABV). Remember that 80 proof is equal to 40 percent ABV.

PRO STORY

Why do we call alcohol content "proof"?

Proof comes from sailors that had a daily ration of rum. To ensure the captain didn't dilute the rum to make it go further, they would make the doctor (who usually doled out the rum rations) light it on fire. The minimum to light is around 80 proof, but higher-alcohol contents will as well. Once the doctor lit the rum, it had been "proofed."

Now that we have the basics of how spirits are made, let's dive into some specific liquors and what makes each of them different.

Vodka: One of the most popular clear spirits, vodka can be made from any raw material and still be considered vodka. That's why we see vodka from lots of different countries because distillers use wheat, rye, potato, corn, or barley to make their brew. After the primary fermentation, they distill the spirit, generally to a higher alcohol level than needed, and then dilute to the target 40 percent ABV. The problem with distilling higher and dilution is that much of the original flavor from the raw materials is lost. The good news is the loss of these flavorful congeners means less hangovers, as we discussed before. Many European and craft vodka producers use a more precise target distillation approach to retain more of the original flavors. Tito's Handmade Vodka uses this precise distillation approach for its vodka and is one of my favorites.

Traditional vodka has no flavors added. Several more modern vodkas have been fancied up with all sorts of citrus and other flavors.

PRO TIP

All vodkas are basically the same.

Roughly 97 percent of the difference in vodka price comes down to branding. I've been told by pros that the best vodka is often the cheapest Russian Standard.

Gin: Gin is like vodka in that it is alcohol that is from a fermented agricultural product, which I know is a broad definition. What makes gin unique is it has a secondary distillation with a combination of botanicals that are placed in a mesh gin basket inside the still. The alcohol in the distillation extracts the flavor elements of the botanicals into the gin. Traditional gin has juniper as the primary flavor element, but all distillers have their own approach. Gibson's and Bombay are good English Dry gins. More modern gins have a variety of botanical flavors with some largely eliminating the traditional juniper.

Whiskey: Whiskey (or whisky) is the most generic amber spirit and can be made from a variety of malted grains, including corn, wheat, rye, and barley. The malting process germinates the grain and then dries it, which turns the starches into fermentable sugars. The malt is then fermented and distilled, usually in a copper still or a distillation column with copper innards to remove the unsavory sulfur compounds.

After distillation, the spirit is placed in oak barrels, like wine. The oak imparts a wonderful smoothness and vanilla elements into the whiskey. The more aging, the smoother the product. Unfortunately, as the whiskey ages, it evaporates at a rate of about 4 percent a year, so it is expensive to age whiskey due to cumulative losses.

If the whiskey is made from a single batch of malt, it is called a single malt, like Yamazaki. If the distiller doesn't want that variation, they will blend multiple batches to get a more uniform flavor profile, called a blended whiskey, like Cutty Sark or J&B. One interesting variant is Irish Whiskey, which is triple filtered to give it unusual smoothness, like Bushmills.

Bourbon: Bourbon is really a subset of whiskey. It contains at least 51 percent corn as the raw material and uses a similar production process to traditional whiskey. Maker's Mark and Woodford Reserve are two mass-market brands. America is the king of corn and so bourbon is considered a largely American product. There is a ton of creativity going on in the craft Bourbon community at the moment.

Scotch: Scotch or Scotch Whisky is also a subset of whiskey with the product coming from Scotland (they remove the "e"). The unique peaty and smoky flavors come from burning peat to dry the malt in the production process. Scotch Whisky is normally double distilled, but some distillers do many additional rounds. The best scotches are single malts that exhibit a tremendous amount of local flavor like Oban or Talisker. Mass production products are blended to give a uniform product like Johnnie Walker in various colors.

Rum: The raw material used for rum is sugarcane molasses or sugarcane juice. It is fermented and distilled and then aged in oak to give it color and smooth the flavor. Rum is available in lighter and darker colors. The darker rums are aged in heavily charred barrels to imbibe the color. Most quality rums come from the Caribbean due to the abundance of sugarcane, but they are available from other regions as well. Bacardi is a brand from Puerto Rico, but I also like Flor de Caña from Costa Rica.

Tequila: Tequila is a distinctly Mexican product, coming from near the town of Tequila. Tequila follows a similar process to other spirits, but the raw ingredient is the blue agave plant. The blue agave is harvested, and the central "piña" is cut out and baked to break down the sugars. These are then mashed, and the juice is sent to be fermented. The product is usually double distilled and then stored in oak barrels to add flavor and mellow the spirit. As we move from Blanco to Reposado to Añejo to Extra Añejo, there will be more oak aging and mellowing, and a darker color from the oak. You'll usually find Patron on the bar shelves, but there are lots of smaller producers too, like Don Julio.

PRO TIP

Tequila only comes from one place.

Like Champagne, if it isn't made from blue agave from the designated area in Mexico of Tequila—it isn't tequila.

In almost all cases, conventional spirits are designed to be consumed with a mixer and make some great cocktails. As we head to the more expensive and aged versions, they are consumed neat (all by themselves) or perhaps just with a little water to open the flavor.

Whatever your preference, remember these spirits start at 40 percent ABV—so watch how many you have!

[9]

MIXOLOGY

YOU MIGHT BE LIKE ME and didn't even know the word mixology existed a few years ago. The idea of applying it to the creation of a craft cocktail is an exciting renaissance in professional drinking. No more rack liquors and bulk manufactured mixes to slop together into an industrial cocktail. It follows the fine dining trend. Why would you precede a wonderful ten-course tasting menu with a cocktail better served at a sorority social?

It isn't actually new; it is a return to basics—no mixes, all-natural ingredients, locally sourced, and handcrafted. This is how cocktails used to be made until we entered the most recent mass-production era. It has unleashed amazing creativity and has rejuvenated long-lost classic cocktails. The basics of any mixed drink are the liquor, the flavoring, the glassware, and the garnish. Let's break them down:

LIQUOR

The spirits behind the bar are normally classified either into the cheap stuff in the speed rack or "call" (as in call a name to order it), which is the stuff higher up on the shelves that goes for higher prices. The spirits being used for high-end cocktails are usually locally sourced and small batch, and many times have unique flavor profiles. They are always call liquors.

Some would argue that the use of such special spirits is a waste; after all, it's getting mixed with other things that mask the flavors. But they'd be wrong. The mixologist may have tasted 20 gins to find the perfect one to make their gin and tonic, with small batch or homemade tonic, and special citrus to finish it off. Many of the popular cocktails have more than one liquor in them, sometimes with a flavoring and sometimes not. These boutique liquors aren't cheap, but like the best ingredients used in the kitchen—it's worth it.

FLAVORING

This is where mixology shines. Small amounts of carefully crafted flavor additives are the key to the perfect cocktail. Most of the mixologists are putting their own spin on a traditional drink, but others create new cocktails, inspired by a new vermouth or a specialty absinthe or an interesting liqueur they found. While the doses may be small, the harmony between the spirit and the flavoring make the magic happen.

I can remember drinking a gin and tonic in a bar in Seville, Spain that contained very high-end gin, a house-made tonic, and an amazing local orange slice. It was probably the best gin and tonic I've ever had, and now I am completely spoiled for supermarket tonic. (Yes, I had a second and it was just as good.) Once you've experienced this kind of thoughtful combination, it is hard to go back.

GLASSWARE

While drinking your mojito out of a red Solo cup is fun at the beach or a concert, it isn't the experience you'll have at a cocktail bar. There are glasses that enhance the flavor or the presentation of any cocktail. When I say martini, a long-stemmed glass with a V-shaped bowl comes to mind. That evokes the elegance of the drink and allows room for the required garnish (three blue cheese olives, in my case). Every drink has a glass that gives the right feel and look. A proper mixologist has a complete supply of clean and elegant glassware to present their creations.

GARNISH

I mentioned my preference for three blue cheese olives in my dry martini, but like the perfect glassware, cocktails have a perfect garnish. To be fair, the definition of perfect is somewhat in the eye of the beholder and an area of creativity for the mixologist. Like the more sophisticated flavors in the drink, the garnish will be carefully selected for flavor profile to complement the beverage and lend a finishing touch. You'll see unique citrus and herbs from exotic locations to complete the experience.

TECHNIQUE

We've all had rum punch with the rum from an unrecognizable producer slammed into a cup as fast as possible and served with a little slosh over the top lip as the bartender slides it across the bar. Mixologists are the exact opposite of this. Ingredients are carefully measured, layered, and combined in a painstaking process to net the best possible drink. Don't be fooled; these techniques have been tested and perfected to put that delicious concoction together. I liken the technique to half surgery and half ballet when it is done at the highest level. You'll be paying a bit more for the drink, so don't miss the show.

PRICE

You knew it was coming, the bill for all this wonderfulness. Specialty cocktails are the fine wine of the bar scene. Each of the ingredients are the best available, and the mixologist is seasoned, educated, and creative. Everything comes together with flair, using the perfect glass and a garnish that makes it all shine. Yes, it will be a bit more expensive than your rack vodka and cranberry juice, but like a fine meal or a fine wine, you are paying for the experience.

PRO TIP

Go for a variation on a classic cocktail.

When I hit a high-end bar, I like to try one of two things. The first is a new drink that the mixologist has created. My problem with this is, if I like the cocktail, I'll never have it again—unless I come back. My preferred approach is to get a classic cocktail, or the mixologist's variation on it. It's great to see their spin, and I have plenty of knowledge of other versions I have tasted to compare it to.

[10]

THE 20 COCKTAILS YOU SHOULD KNOW (AND TRY)

MIXOLOGY HAS BROUGHT A RISE of the celebrity bartender and the use of local fresh ingredients. I think that's a great thing and offers a chance to have some fun with a cocktail before we head to dinner and wine. Most of these drinks are not designed to pair with food, but rather they are meant to be enjoyed stand-alone.

Even with the explosion of cocktails and craft cocktails, they generally follow the structure of a drink listed below. I picked 20 cocktails that can certainly be called classic, but it would be easy to argue that more deserve to make the list and I wouldn't object.

If you are feeling a little adventurous, pick one that looks compelling and give it a try the next time you are out. A warning: If you are in a beer-and-shot kind of bar, the bartender might not know some of these cocktails. I wouldn't recommend being their maiden voyage on a new drink!

Old Fashioned: My father loved his old fashioned, and it is a drink that has lasted through the ages. It's comprised of rye whiskey or bourbon, a sugar cube soaked in bitters, and an orange twist. It's usually poured over a single large ice cube to limit dilution.

Negroni: Negroni is a favorite cocktail of the Sommelier class and those that spent time in Italy. It packs a punch with a mixture of gin, Campari bitters, and vermouth.

Manhattan: A Manhattan evokes the sophistication of this epic city. The drink is simple and timeless, basically a martini with rye whiskey, sweet vermouth, and bitters with a cherry to garnish. There is a whole debate on the best Manhattan, usually pitting rye versus bourbon and sweet against dry vermouth, or a mixture as polarizing positions to be argued for hours at bars around the country.

Dry Martini: If you want to feel like a grown-up, order a dry martini. I like them up and ice cold to the point of some ice forming on the surface. London dry gin is the primary ingredient, with a little vermouth and garnished with olives on a toothpick. Upgrade to blue cheese-stuffed olives for a treat.

Margarita: The margarita is another simple thirst quencher. Blanco tequila, lime juice, and triple sec are shaken and poured over ice. It's perfect for a hot day. The frozen version was invented in Dallas and often comes from a mix with less than pure ingredients, which can be real hangover inducers. (I'm speaking from personal experience here.)

Bloody Mary: A meal in a cocktail, the Bloody Mary is a brunch favorite and a well-regarded hangover cure. Everyone fools with the recipe, but it involves tomato juice (hey, it's healthy!), spices like black pepper, Tabasco, horseradish (my personal favorite), and vodka as the spirit. The garnishes range from celery to olives and even candied bacon.

Sazerac: Originating in New Orleans in the 1800s, this drink gets the party rolling. Rye or brandy is combined with turbinado sugar syrup, bitters, and a lemon twist. If you can get some absinthe, a little makes the drink and gives it that speakeasy feel, since absinthe was illegal in America until 2007.

Mojito: You can't spell Cuba without mojito. It's one of the island's best contributions to global culture. The drink consists of white rum, cane sugar, and lime juice, all muddled with fresh mint. It's another perfect summer drink.

Boulevardier: Like a Negroni, this might be the second most popular drink among Sommeliers. Rye whiskey, amaro, and sweet vermouth are combined and garnished with an orange twist. It is elegant and packs a punch.

French 75: French 75 is a cocktail made from gin, Champagne, lemon juice, and sugar. The drink dates to World War I and was reputed to make your head pound like you were near a French 75-millimeter cannon. It debuted in 1915 at the New York Bar in Paris.

Cosmopolitan: The Cosmopolitan or Cosmo can thank Sarah Jessica Parker for its popularity when her character, Carrie, drank it regularly on *Sex in the City*. It's a delicious combination of vodka, triple sec, cranberry juice, and lime juice. Usually served up, the pink color gets the party started.

Vodka Martini: Like the more popular dry gin martini, the vodka martini is simple and strong. It's made with a shot of well-chilled vodka shaken with a spritz of dry vermouth and garnished with an olive. It's a strong statement for the start of the evening and popular at business events. Perhaps that's why Hollywood places the iconic martini glass in front of everyone from CEOs to international super spies.

Tom Collins: One of my early favorite summer drinks, the Tom Collins combines gin, lemon, and soda water. It makes for a fizzy quencher with a little more interest than its brother, the gin and tonic.

Daiquiri: The traditional daiquiri is a simple combination of white rum, lime juice, and simple syrup over lots of ice. A perfect beach drink, in my opinion.

Long Island Iced Tea: If you want to party like it's 1985, then jump into a Long Island iced tea. This potent concoction masks the punch of multiple spirits with a dose of sweet cola. The bartender combines vodka, tequila, rum, gin, and triple sec (sometimes pouring them at the same time), then finishes with Coke from the fountain. This one really isn't appropriate in the business setting.

Vesper: If you can't decide on a gin or vodka martini, don't, and grab a Vesper. Ian Fleming made this drink famous in his book *Casino Royale* with vodka, gin, and vermouth (preferably Lillet) and garnished with a lemon peel.

Aperol Spritz: Cocktails have their moment and fade, and the aperol spritz is currently on the rise. It's a delicious summer quaff. You combine prosecco (Italian bubbly white wine), orange flavor aperol, and soda water. It's fizzy and lower alcohol, so you can sip a few of these without trouble. The aperol spritz is a great starter to the evening. But like white shoes, you should probably move on to another drink come Labor Day.

Paloma: If you are hankering for tequila and don't want a margarita, the paloma is your cocktail. It combines tequila, lime juice, a pinch of salt, and grapefruit soda. Tart and a little sweet, it is a wonderful drink to wake up your taste buds.

Moscow Mule: While the aperol spritz might be on the rise, the Moscow mule is probably on the wane. There is no denying the cool factor of the traditional copper mugs that are used for this drink, and everyone knows what you are tucking into from across the bar. This mix of vodka, lime juice, and ginger beer is usually garnished with a lime wedge.

Irish Coffee: Cocktails are usually before a meal, but I felt I needed to include the Irish coffee—but maybe that's my heritage speaking. I love to have an Irish coffee at the end of a meal in place of dessert. Sweet and warm, it's a great way to end the evening. Irish Whiskey is combined with coffee, sugar, and cream to make this sticky sweet drink, and it's usually topped with whipped cream, because... why not?

While this list seems long, it is by no means comprehensive. There are hundreds of variants that are worth a try. With the rise of the sophisticated mixologist at higher-end restaurants, one of my favorite questions is to ask for the signature cocktail or their best version of a classic cocktail, and I am rarely disappointed.

[11]

WHAT YOUR COCKTAIL CHOICE SAYS ABOUT YOU

IT CAN BE TOTALLY APPROPRIATE to order a cocktail at a professional drinking event. Just be prepared for your drink choice to tell other attendees a lot about you.

- Martini—James Bond
- Manhattan—Sophisticate
- Mimosa—Brunch fan
- Mojito—Ready for vacation
- Margarita—On vacation
- Negroni—Somm or wannabe Somm
- Sazerac—Mardi Gras
- Old Fashion—Your father's drink
- Vesper—Ready to play Baccarat in Monaco
- Gin and Tonic—Summer at the yacht club
- Rye and Whiskey—Country club drink
- Rum and Coke—College frat party (senior year)
- French 75—World War I aficionado.
- Mint Julip—Southern belle or horseracing fan (needs a fancy hat)
- Cosmopolitan—Likes martinis, just not the taste
- Neat Scotch—Direct, and possibly Scottish
- Shot and a Beer—Hey, cowboy!
- Shots of anything—No, no, no

[12]

GOING GLOBAL: DRINKING WHAT THE LOCALS DRINK

WHILE THIS BOOK IS PRIMARILY about the professional drinking culture that we have in America, which is dominated by cocktails, wine, and beer, a good rule of thumb is always to drink what the locals are drinking. Here is a quick drive-by through a few different drinking cultures around the world.

England: The English are a pub society; there is a culture of drinking in the pub with their mates. Almost everyone has a local pub that they can walk to from their home. If you get invited to "their local," you are making it inside the circle of trust. They like their cellar temperature ales like John Courage and London Pride. While Americans tend to skew toward a frosty cold mug of beer, you should try the local fare. I can vouch for the fact that when the locals claim their local brewer's beer doesn't give you a hangover (as they will), they are lying.

France: The French drink wine as part of every meal. I remember dining at a restaurant in Paris and even the 13-year-olds were drinking wine. At one business lunch along the Seine in Paris, I was offered wine, which I normally don't drink at lunch. But since I was in France, I did and it quickly became clear how wonderful this tradition is, even when doing business. Be sure to drink locally, as wine is made all over France. You'll get some fun surprises that will perfectly match your meal.

Germany: This country is known for a strong beer culture that has created exacting purity standards that result in fabulous lagers—though the Germans do make some delicious Riesling wines, too. You'll find chilled glasses of precisely poured drafts with paper doilies at the bottom for drip control. I always go for the local draft as it immerses me in the culture and is usually fresh. Be sure to offer the traditional, "Prost!" as you imbibe.

Italy: In Italy, they say wine is food. And they're not kidding; it is part of every single meal. In fact, Italian wines are designed to be eaten with food rather than drunk by themselves. During lunch and dinner, you will be offered wine with the meal to enhance the food. Some of my favorite memories of wine and food in Italy involve a pitcher of the simple house red wine, drawn from a cask in the cellar and brought right to my table. It wasn't fancy, but it was local and perfectly complemented the meal the chef had created. What is exceptionally cool in Italy is that you'll never see 75 percent of the wines you try there in America; they don't have the level of production that merits exporting.

Spain: In Spain, wine is well integrated into the culture and the cuisine. You'll be offered a quaffable local wine at most places and you should indulge and offer your dining companions, "Salud!" The local reds and whites are usually incredible and worth sampling. My beverage of choice is sherry with tapas in the evening in Spain. I admit, I am not the biggest sherry fan when drinking it alone, but with food—wow—it is a magical beverage.

Russia: There's one drink that dominates in Russia: vodka. You will drink it all night long, cheering each other with, "Nostrovia" until you are drunk, so be wary.

China: Everyone likes to drink beer with their Chinese food—including the Chinese. The Chinese also drink Baijiu, which is the most consumed distilled spirit in the world, as an after-dinner drink. It's made from sorghum and, be careful, it's like firewater! The cheers here is "Ganbei," which literally means bottoms up.

That said, the Chinese are up-and-comers when it comes to making wine. They have hired some of the best winemakers on the planet to teach them to grow high-quality grapes. It won't be long before you are sipping some decent Chinese wine with your friends.

Japan: The Japanese are fans of Sapporo or Asahi beer and sake, which is rice wine. While the beer is good, the Sake is incredibly varied and has 1,000 years of tradition with hundreds of local makers. It is a great way to connect to the culture. There is a fine dining scene in Japan, but the wines you will find there are all imported. There are also several good and smooth Japanese whiskies like Suntory, which are usually enjoyed after dinner with some water while businesspeople sing karaoke. You'll say cheers with, "Kanpai!"

Korea: Koreans also enjoy drinking beer followed by Soju, a drink made from fermented rice. Be careful with this innocuous-looking liquid—it is strong!

Part Three
WINE TIME

[13]

THE BASICS OF GRAPES

WHEN IT COMES TO MAKING wine, there are only two kinds of grapes: red and white. In most cases, the juices from both red and white grapes is clear. To make red wines, as well as rosé, you mix in the skins of the grape to add color and flavor and filter them out once you have the color you want. Rosé is red wine with less exposure to the red skins.

Just like any alcohol, wine is the product of sugar, water, and yeast—which, when fermented, results in alcohol and carbon dioxide (bubbles). It's the grapes that provide the sugar. When winemakers harvest grapes, they're looking for a ripeness in the grape that will add to the flavor of the wine. There can be limits to how ripe and juicy grapes can get based on where they are grown. In Germany, for example, there's a much shorter growing season. Vineyards are typically placed in southern-facing slopes to get as much sun exposure as they can during the growing season. In some cases, they even place vineyards in areas with black or gray slate to help absorb and radiate heat to keep the vines warm at night.

THE SEVEN NOBLE GRAPES

The most basic wine knowledge involves an understanding of a very limited set of what are called Noble Grapes or International Varietals.

These are the grapes that make the dominant proportion of fine wines around the world. This is partially because these grapes are hardy enough to grow in most wine climates and they happen to make some excellent juice. Now, this set of seven grapes is just scratching the surface of grapes used to make great wine. We could easily add another dozen popular grapes. Even at 20 grapes, realize that Italy alone has over 3,000 indigenous grapes that are used to make wine, so it depends how far you want to extend your knowledge. For now, we are going to focus on seven grapes.

The Seven Noble Grapes are:

- Chardonnay
- Sauvignon Blanc
- Riesling
- Cabernet Sauvignon
- Pinot Noir
- Merlot
- Syrah

You've probably had wine made from each of these grapes; they exist in almost every significant wine-growing country. What changes in a Chardonnay from France when compared to one from Napa? It's the growing conditions and the impact of the climate and the terroir (or the local expression of the earth). It can be great fun to try two bottles of the same grape grown in different parts of the world to see the impact. This is one of the techniques sommeliers use when blind tasting to determine where a grape was grown.

Let's dig into each grape a bit more:

Chardonnay: This thin-skinned grape makes for relatively light wine. Nicely aromatic when grown in a warm climate, like Napa, California, more austere when grown in a cool climate, like France. You'll find Chardonnay-based wine from France (Chablis, Champagne, Burgundy), South America, Australia, and California (Sonoma, Napa). Because it is grown in so many places, Chardonnay makes very different wines based on the conditions. You can serve it across a meal in the different styles and have some fun.

Sauvignon Blanc: These are thin-skinned grapes with intense aromatics. The most distinct aromas are gooseberries and cut grass. It is grown in France (Loire, Bordeaux), New Zealand, California, Italy, Chile, and South Africa. Sauvignon Blanc is a bracing wine that is wonderful as a summer drink or with lightly flavored foods.

Riesling: This is an intensely aromatic grape that has a lot of skin influence due to the small grapes, which have more skin per volume of juicy interior pulp. Rieslings are grown in Germany, France (Alsace), Italy, Austria, Australia, New York State, and Canada. Many times, it is made into sweeter versions (although not always) by harvesting late in the season. These are elegant wines that are probably underserved because people think they are sweet. The best versions are bone dry and every sip leaves you wanting more. Rieslings are a favorite of sommeliers, so if you ask them what they drink, you'll likely end up with a nice dry Riesling from Germany.

Cabernet Sauvignon: Cabernet Sauvignon is considered the king of red grapes and makes some of the most expressive and powerful wines around. These are thick-skinned grapes that make an opaque wine with intense flavors from the grapes and the typical oak aging. You'll find Cabernet Sauvignon in France (Bordeaux), Napa, Washington, Australia, Italy, Spain, South Africa, and Chile. It also forms the base for some of the best blended wines on the planet from Bordeaux and Napa.

Pinot Noir: This thin-skinned grape makes for lightly colored wines with delicate flavors of non-fruit elements. You'll find this difficult-to-grow grape in France (Burgundy, Champagne), Oregon, California, New Zealand, and Chile. If you've seen *Sideways*, you may remember Miles talking about the elegance of the Pinot Noir grape, and he is right. The Pinot Noir grape makes elegant and sophisticated wines that can age for decades.

Merlot: If Cabernet Sauvignon is the king, Merlot is the queen of red grapes. It makes less aggressive, smoother, easier drinking wines with great subtlety and flavors. It's a thick-skinned grape that produces a deeply colored wine. It can be used alone or as a blending element with Cabernet Sauvignon, where it adds a softening and suppleness to the wine. It is most popular in France (Bordeaux), Italy, California, Washington, Australia, South Africa, and Chile.

Syrah: Syrah is one of the gateway wines for many people, as it is a jammy, wonderful wine from Australia. These thick-skinned grapes make intensely colored wines. Syrah or Shiraz, as they call it in Australia, has a range of expressions from elegant and refined with lots of non-fruit notes to fruit bombs with high alcohol. We find Syrah in France (Northern Rhone), Australia, California (Paso Robles), and Washington.

If you want to get a start on your wine knowledge, keep it simple and taste your way through these seven grapes from a variety of locations. You'll probably find something new you like and get a better appreciation for the versatility of these amazing grapes.

PRO TIP

European vines aren't that old.

Originally, cuttings were taken from European vines—known as "noble" grapes—and brought to America, where they became the foundation for U.S. winemaking regions like California. But then at some point, when Californian wines began to become popular, a Frenchman took cuttings and brought them back to France. What he didn't know, however, was that he also brought along a stowaway: a kind of aphid called Phylloxera that lived in the roots. While the American grapevines had developed a resistance to the pest, the French vines were entirely wiped out. In order to replant the devastated French vineyards, they transplanted rootstock from American grapevines with resistance. When you drink French wine today, you're sampling wine made from vines transplanted from America. (which were originally from France).

[14]

MAKING WINE

MAKING WINE STARTS WITH GRAPES and more specifically, ripe grapes. The secret of the grower is to bring the grapes to their ultimate peak of ripeness, given their local weather and geography. The trick is to pick them as ripe as possible before colder weather or storms that can ruin a harvest arrive. This means the grapes have the most sugar possible, and that's what the winemaker needs to produce a great wine.

Grapes need sun to ripen, so most grapes are grown closer to the equator on the southern and northern hemispheres. But you don't want to be too close. The ideal spot is somewhere between the 30th and 50th latitude in the northern and southern hemisphere. When you're closer to the equator, like southern France, you get riper grapes with more sugar content. When you're farther away, like northern Germany, that means less ripeness and fewer sugars in the grapes. The grape grower will measure the sugar content using an optical tool called a refractometer that measures the juice and tells the brix, which roughly translates to the percentage of sugar in the juice. Seasoned growers can taste a few grapes and predict the sugar content very closely; the machine just verifies what they already know.

Sugar is important because during fermentation the yeast will consume the sugar and turn it into alcohol. The more sugar there is for the yeast to process, the higher the alcohol content. Two sugar molecules are used to make one alcohol molecule. That means grapes with 26 percent sugar will yield approximately a 13 percent alcohol wine, if all the sugar is processed, which it is in typical dry wines. Therefore, most wines, on average, have about 12 to 15 percent alcohol. Without it, we'd just be drinking fancy grape juice.

But that 13 percent is just an average. In some wines, the winemaker will stop the fermentation earlier, not using all the sugar in the juice they have collected. This means that the alcohol content will be lower. German Rieslings use this approach to make some of their sweeter versions. The technical term for this is residual sugar, or RS if you're a wine geek.

The other factor to consider is the body of the wine. We can see the body of a wine when we swirl our glass and watch the tears slide down the side of the glass. When the tears run quickly down, the wine is lighter body. Thick, slow tears indicate a heavier body wine. What causes body? Alcohol and residual sugar. Some wines have a lot of body because they have lots of alcohol, 14 percent or higher. Other wines have body due to a lower alcohol content, but a fair dose of residual sugar. You won't know which one until you taste it.

So why wouldn't a winemaker grow anywhere but closer to the equator, to ensure they get maximum ripeness? The answer is acid. We've all tasted a fruit when it is under-ripe and get that pucker factor. This acid can be desirable in many wines, like crisp whites or reds that can pair wonderfully with food. Winemakers make the best use of the grapes they can grow, giving the drinker a balance between alcohol, residual sugar, body, and acid. If the grapes were grown too close to the equator, the wines would be super high alcohol, taste a bit like stewed fruit, and lack the acid to balance the alcohol and sugar.

The next time you drink some of your favorite wine, think about the grapes, how ripe they must have been, and where they were grown to get the alcohol level and the acid you experience.

[15]

OLD WORLD VS. NEW WORLD WINES

IF YOU HANG AROUND WINE people, you'll hear them talk about New World vs. Old World wines. It seems like a simple phase, but it has meaning for taste and other factors when you drink each of these wines.

Larger-scale wine production started with the Greeks and Romans, and they brought their winemaking knowledge with them as they conquered the areas around the Mediterranean. The Middle East, France, and Spain all benefited from the Romans and their knowledge. They had good reason for this: the water wasn't safe to drink. But if you turned it into wine, the troops wouldn't get sick. The Romans made sure there was wine everywhere they went. And if it wasn't there, they planted it. Now wine from this era is mostly called Old World.

New World wines come from more recently developed areas and areas that came to the wine game later, well after the Roman expansion. America, Chile, Argentina, Australia, and New Zealand are the typical New World wine regions.

Most of the Seven Noble Grapes are grown in regions around the world; Cabernet Sauvignon, Merlot, Chardonnay, and Syrah (or Shiraz) can be found in almost every wine-growing country. Of course, there are also usually dozens of indigenous grapes that have very local flavor and character.

Beyond where the grapes are grown, the differences in what you smell and taste in Old World and New World wines comes down to fruit and non-fruit. We've all heard those wine snobs bloviate about the slightly tart Macintosh apple or charred blood orange smells they pick up when they plunge their nose into a freshly poured glass of wine. I used to be a skeptic. In fact, I have accused more than a few friends of making it all up.

When you smell a wine, just ask a simple question: Is the first thing I smell fruit? Lemon, apple, cherry, or plums, for example. Or is it something that is non-fruit? Like herbs, vanilla, stone, petrol, or barnyard. This simple test can give you a lot of information on the wine. You have basically categorized the wine into New World and Old World with one sniff.

Generally, New World wines like those from Australia and California are going to be fruit forward, and the fruit will be the first thing you smell and taste. Old World wines will have non-fruit aromas on the nose and a similar taste profile. That is not to say that Old World wines don't have fruit—they do. But it tends to be more restrained, along for the ride versus driving the bus.

If you want to impress your friends, smell, and taste some wine without seeing the label. And see if you can call out New World or Old World with this simple approach.

PRO STORY

The 1976 Judgment in Paris

A fun story you can share at your next professional drinking event is how American wines first became accepted on the world stage. It dates back to 1976 when Steven Spurrier, a British wine merchant living in Paris, was trying to drum up interest in Californian wines—which were, at that time, still considered inferior to the Old-World wines. He set up a blind tasting in Paris where a panel of French wine experts would choose the best from a series of French and American wines. You can probably guess what happened next: the French wine experts picked both a California Chardonnay from Château Montelena and a California Cabernet

Sauvignon from Stag's Leap Wine Cellars as the winners—which forever changed the way the wine world looked at American grapes.

[16]

A QUICK OVERVIEW OF THE WINE WORLD

WHEN YOU DRINK WINE FROM different areas of the world, you can almost think of them as different personalities. Who do you want to have dinner with tonight?

France: The granddaddy of wine. A traditionalist. They've forgotten more than you know, but they make great stuff.

Italy: Like your lovable uncle who's just a little bit different. He'll try making wine with grapes you've never heard of before in his backyard. There are 3,000 indigenous grapes in Italy—you can't taste them all in a lifetime. Italian wine is designed to be consumed with food, so it's usually a good choice at a meal.

Spain: This is like your other crazy uncle, the one who tries new things nobody ever had before and continues to innovate and modernize their wine industry. They are not bound by tradition.

Germany: This is like your professor next door with a tweed jacket who does everything with precision and perfection. Everything is organized and ordered, which is why they're able to make delicious, difficult wines like Riesling in their cooler climate.

Argentina: These wines are like your hot-blooded friend, the one who is always the life of the party, shows up at 10 p.m. and leaves at 4 a.m. Bolder and fuller, they have more refined products coming from the higher altitudes.

America: These wines are your nouveau niche; they have money and they know it. They're flashy, especially if they're from Napa Valley, where they'll likely sport fancy labels and high price points. The wine is good, but it comes with attitude.

Australia: This is another risk-taker. They grow crazy grapes and try new things. They don't follow rules to get there; it's all about outcomes. It's all fun, and they don't take themselves too seriously.

Chile: This is your up-and-comer; the new guest at the party. Keep an eye on them as they promise to mature and get better over time. Still a great value now.

[17]

WINE NAMING: GRAPES OR PLACES?

YUP, IT'S CONFUSING. SOMETIMES A wine is named by the grape used to make it and sometimes it is named by the area where it is grown. Lots of times, there is no indication of the grape used to make the wine on the label in this second group; you are just supposed to know.

So how does this break down and what are the few things you might want to remember?

If a wine is a New World Wine, grown basically anywhere outside of Europe, it will be named by the grape used to make the wine. But like all things in wine, there are some exceptions, including fancy marketing names and certain blends. But you should be able to find the grapes used to make the wine somewhere on the label.

PRO TIP

New World wines are usually named for the grape used.

That means American, Australian, Chilean, Argentinian, and other New World locales will primarily use the grape to define their product. Good examples would be an Oregon Pinot Noir, a Napa Cabernet Sauvignon, and a Chilean Chardonnay. It's simple to order—name the grape and the country and your sommelier can find something you will like easily.

When we move to the Old World, things get more complex. Most of Europe uses the location of the vineyard to name their wines. This includes France, Italy, Portugal, and Spain, the larger wine producers in the Old World. That means you must remember what grape is grown where to get what you'd like.

PRO TIP

Old World wines are named for the location, mostly.

Here is a simple summary (and it is not a complete set) of a few wines and where in the Old World they are grown:

Grape	Country	Typical Regions
Chardonnay (White)	France	Chablis Burgundy Champagne
Sauvignon Blanc (White)	France Italy	Loire Valley Northern Italy and Tuscany
Riesling (White)	France Germany	Alsace Germany
Cabernet Sauvignon (Red)	France Italy	Bordeaux (Left Bank) Super Tuscans (Bolgheri)
Pinot Noir (Red)	France Germany	Burgundy Champagne Spatburgunder (Ahn)
Merlot (Red)	France Italy	Bordeaux (Right Bank) Super Tuscans (Bolgheri)
Syrah (Red)	France Italy	Northern Rhone Tuscany (Cortona)

It's also worth noting that I am only describing some of the classic locations and the classic grapes. There is always experimentation going on, and grapes are being grown in new locations to see if they make a great wine.

One of the main grapes that gets confused is Chardonnay. Diners will ask for a Chardonnay, and when the sommelier proposes a nice Chablis, they reject it, forgetting that Chablis is made from the Chardonnay grape. Who could blame them? Sommeliers take years to accumulate all the knowledge of grapes and locations and flavor profiles. It's not fair to expect someone with a life outside wine to recall it all.

PRO TIP

Chablis is Chardonnay, just grown in the Chablis area of France.

Two notable exceptions to the idea that Old World wines use location to name their wines are Rieslings from Germany and the wines of the Alsace region of France. Both regions are nice enough to name their product by the grape. You will find German Rieslings, with clear indications of the location of the vineyard, because it does matter to the quality of the wine. Alsace, perhaps because of the German influences over the years, also uses grape names for their world-class Riesling, Gewürztraminer, Pinot Gris, Pinot Blanc, Muscat, and Pinot Noir. Both Germany and Alsace also indicate a more precise vineyard location as the quality of the wine increases.

Like I said, it is confusing. Keep things simple by remembering two big rules:

1. **Old World uses places to name wines, and New World uses grapes (except for the exceptions).**
2. **Chablis is a Chardonnay.**

[18]

THE 100-POINT WINE SCALE

YOU'LL SEE WINE RATINGS IN wine shops, but many restaurants will also list them next to their wines on the list. It's worth understanding what goes into a wine rating.

In wine shops, wines usually have scores in the 80s or even 90s. But what do these scores really mean? Are higher-scoring wines definitively better? And how are the scores derived?

The first thing to realize is that the 100-point score is more like a 30-point scale from 70 to 100. And almost no winery would boast of its amazing 72-point wine. It's like bragging you got a C- on a test.

Is a wine with a 90 rating better than a wine with an 86 rating? Well, that depends. Different critics have different palates. And one might rate a wine more highly because it fits their taste profile. The big ratings operations are *Wine Spectator*, *Wine Advocate*, and *Wine Enthusiast*. These are shortened to WS, WA, and WE, respectively, when the ratings are shown in the store. In my experience, WE is the easiest grader with WS being harder and WA being the hardest grader for the same wine.

Wine Spectator magazine, one of the largest wine scoring operations, indicates the following qualitative rating by score:

- 95-100 wines are benchmark examples or classic
- 90-94 wines are superior to exceptional
- 85-90 wines are good to very good
- 80-84 wines are above average to good

- 70-79 wines are flawed and taste average
- 60-69 wines are flawed and not recommended

The distribution of wine ratings from *Wine Spectator* from 2009-2013 shows an average rating of about 88, with very few wines below 81 and only slightly more above 94.

PRO TIP

The average rating for a wine is 88 points, a B+. No one brags about getting a C- on a report card.

The other factor is the rating is relative to other wines of that type. A 95-point Syrah tastes different than a 95-point Riesling. A high score like that means it is a great example of that kind of wine from that area. And you might prefer one over the other, without regard to the rating.

Ever wonder why you don't see those 70-point-rated wines? Lots of them are never tasted. In fact, most wines are not rated and that's okay—it doesn't make them bad wines. But if they were scored and did poorly, their marketers won't be talking about it.

How do the scorers come up with the rating? The current 100-point scale was popularized by wine critic Robert Parker of *Wine Advocate* and derived from an earlier 20-point system from UC Davis.

The scoring goes like this:

Factor	Comments	Potential Score
It's wine	Like signing your name on the SAT—everyone gets this	50
Color and appearance	How the wine looks; optics	5

Aroma and bouquet	What the nose perceives; complexity	15
Flavor and finish	What you taste and length of the finish	20
Overall quality	Subjective factor: integrated experience	10
Total Available		100

While this appears simple, it requires a trained palate to differentiate on each of these scales. It's quite hard to get a high score on this evaluation as a lot of things must be done right. The 100-point scale took over and most rating organizations use it at this point. You will occasionally see a wine rated on a 20-point scale. While it isn't exact, I just multiply by five to translate.

Over time, some winemakers have learned how to prep for the test and try to deliver wines that are designed to score well. In some cases, they have learned the taste profile of some famous tasters and shifted their wines to be pleasing to them. This has been called "Parkerization" in honor of Robert Parker, an influential wine rater.

Should you always look for highly rated wines? My advice is to find areas of the world and grapes that you prefer and maybe even some specific estates that have a house style you prefer. If you want to chase scores within that area, go for it. Just realize you can't compare an 88-point Napa Cabernet with an 88-point French Champagne. Also realize this has become more of a marketing effort than an effort to make amazing wines, so take it all with a grain of salt.

PRO TIP

Good wine is one you enjoy.

When people ask me if a wine is a good wine, my response is to ask if they enjoy it. If they do, I respond, "Then it's good wine."

Wine is about what you like, not what the critics say. We've all seen a show that the critics didn't love, but we enjoyed immensely. Wine is the same way.

[19]

THE DIFFERENCE BETWEEN A $10 AND $100 BOTTLE OF WINE

YOU CAN SPEND A WIDELY varying amount on a bottle of wine, from a bottle of Barefoot wine at less than $5 to a bottle of Château Petrus at nearly $5,000. They are both wine, made from grapes, so what causes this difference? And what goes into the costs?

Land: The first element of cost in any wine is the land that the grapes are grown on. Inexpensive wine is grown in large plots of very inexpensive land. On the flip side, pricey wine is grown on expensive land. A few years ago, land in the premium wine-growing region of Burgundy in France for Grand Cru vineyards was going for around $5 million an acre. You can't grow anything cheap when the land is that expensive.

Grapes: The grapes that are used for the wine are also important and particularly the yield of the grapes in tons per acre. Some grapes are notoriously lower yielding, while inexpensive wines use hardy grapes that can resist almost anything and still yield lots of juice.

Vineyard Management: The structure of the vineyard, including spacing and irrigation, also plays into the yield of the grapes. If you want perfect grapes for an expensive wine, there will be plenty of airflow and sunlight for your little darlings. And regular hand pruning of the vines is necessary to remove poor clusters and leaves that are excessively shading the grapes. Bulk wine operations do no hand pruning; they want every grape, so they grow densely planted grapes in rich, fertile ground to maximize the yield. While a high-end vineyard might yield one to two tons of grapes per acre, a mass-production vineyard might be eight to ten tons per acre or higher.

Harvest: Premium grapes are hand harvested when they are at the peak of ripeness. This can mean growers make multiple passes through the vineyard, selecting only those perfect clusters that are ready. They are then carefully handled to prevent bruising of the fruit on the way to the crushers. Large-scale operations might make a single pass through the vines using giant machines to harvest all the grapes, imperfect or not, by shaking them off the vine, tossing them into a big bin, and hauling them away for processing.

Premium estates might yield two tons of grapes or less an acre with bulk wines yielding many times this amount. A ton of grapes yields around 720 bottles of wine, so that's roughly only 1,440 bottles per acre—with some super-premium wines well below this figure. As an example, you can buy grapes grown for bulk wine at $340 a ton, while a ton of premium Napa grapes will set you back more than $3,600.

Squeezing the Grapes: Once the grapes have been harvested, the juice is pressed out. In the first pressing, or "free-run," the juice comes out with the first gentle squeeze of the grapes and is used for the best wines. Bulk wines will press much harder and many times to extract every drop of juice from the grapes they have. Some premium wines will use the second pressing to make a lesser wine that they will sell under a different name.

Oak: Most premium red wines and some white wines are aged in oak barrels to impart tannins and give a depth of flavor to the wine. These barrels don't come cheap! New American oak might cost $1,000 for a smaller 225-liter barrel and around $2,500 for a new French oak barrel of the same size. These barrels fit around 300 bottles of wine, and some premium makers only use them once before they are turned into flowerpots.

Operation: The grape juice, once pressed, will spend 18 to 24 months being converted into the wine the producer wants to sell. During this time, they still have to pay for the building, labor, rent, insurance, lighting, and so forth. Bulk operations look more like a chemical plant with stainless steel plumbing and a relatively short residence time in the winery.

Bottle, Cork, and Label: An eye-catching label and pretty bottle can help sell a wine. For a bulk wine, this means a thinner bottle with a cute label and an inexpensive seal, perhaps screwcap. Premium wines will have elegant labels, sometimes with original artwork from a famous artist, a heavy glass bottle designed to hold up for extended cellaring, and a premium cork with tight structure and extra length. The bottle can easily run $3 to $4 and the cork another $3.

Labor: A lot of labor is required to run a vineyard, from the farmer to the pruners to the harvesters. Once inside the winery, there is production help and a very expensive winemaker in the middle. Since winemakers need certain types of talent at the same time, the price for these services gets bid up substantially.

Marketing: Finally, we get to the X-factor: marketing. Any good marketer will tell you that there isn't a correlation between price and cost. Price is set by the market and what people will pay. While the bulk wine companies are focused on the lower end of the market and price that way, the premium producers go over the top on every element of the winemaking process. When they finally set price, the market demand and the perception of the wine come into play. No matter the costs they have put into the bottle, the market will set the price. In the case of super-premium Napa reds and French burgundies that clock in at $1000 a bottle, it can make you dizzy (and that's before you drink it)!

[20]

IS THIS A GOOD WINE?

IS THIS A GOOD WINE? It is the anxious question many people ask themselves when they select something from a wine list. Remember what I said in the beginning of this book: There is no bad wine! It just depends on where and with whom you're drinking it. And if the wine list is properly curated, there won't be any "bad" wines; a restaurant's sommelier or general manager will have tasted every single selection and approved it. Often, it becomes a question of choosing the wine that pairs best with your meal. So, relax, take a deep breath, and repeat "wine is fun" to yourself.

PRO TIP

P/Q ratio is more important than price.

Ultimately, the ratio of the price to the quality or the P/Q ratio is more important than the price. There are great wines for $10, when you consider the price. They probably won't be as good as a well-made $100 bottle, but you'll be $90 ahead of the game too. The point is that your P/Q ratio can help set expectations for what you want out of your wine.

Frankly, PQ is a bit subjective. As an engineer, I find it frustrating that I can't plug something into a formula and crank out a relative value measurement. You know the price of the bottle, so we have a number to work with there, but the quality of the wine is more subjective. Luckily, the experts have given us a way to think about quality.

PRO TIP

The professionals use BLIC to determine wine quality.

The main measurement you can use in judging your wine is something professionals call **BLIC**—an acronym for balance, length, intensity, and complexity. Let's break it down:

- **Balance:** This relates to how balanced the wine is between sweetness, tannins, acid, and alcohol. It's a question of how harmonious the wine is—or isn't. If it is all acid or all fruit without any balancing elements, that is usually considered an inferior wine (unless you like it that way).
- **Length:** Length is a measure of how long the taste of the wine lingers on your tongue after you've sipped it. Does it have a simple note that goes away quickly, something that you might enjoy on a hot summer day on the back porch? Or does it have a serious length where it lingers for 20, 30, or even 60 seconds on your tongue? A longer length is indicative of a great wine.
- **Intensity:** What happens when you smell the wine? What about the flavors? Is it more profound in the aromas, with layer after layer of fruit, non-fruit, organic, and inorganic odors? The same should happen when you taste it, with intense and interesting flavors that unwrap on your tongue. Or is it more simple, thin, and lacking in this power?
- **Complexity:** Does the wine have simple notes, like the taste of lemon and apples? Or is it more complex, where you can detect flavors like tobacco, leather, forest floor, cedar, vanilla, and slate? Does it evoke memories and feeling as you smell and drink it? More layers and complexity make for a better wine and a better drinking experience. While there is a place for a single-note wine, they generally are not considered as good.

Again, the point is that it's somewhat arbitrary to decide whether a wine is "good" or not. But if you decide to splurge for a bottle with a high P/Q ratio, you should also expect it to shine on the BLIC scale relative to the price.

[21]

WHAT'S BETTER, SCREW CAP OR CORK?

IT'S A QUESTION AS OLD as screw caps (corks have been around a while). And the simple answer is: it depends. Some wines are just better in one or the other. Ultimately, it's a winemaker's choice. Let's look at the differences.

CORK

Cork has been the preferred closure for wine bottles since the late 1600s, when winemakers developed the ability to make relatively uniform glass bottles in volume.

Cork is made from the bark of the cork oak tree. The bark grows thick and spongy. Experts use blades to carefully remove the thick bark in sheets without damaging the underlying tree materials. The bark then grows back over a period of seven to nine years, just in time for another harvest. Most of the corks used in commercial production are from Portugal and a bit from Spain. The corks we know are then punched from the cork bark, cleaned, labeled, and sent to the bottler.

The cork has a wonderful pliable nature that allows the bottler to squeeze the cork into the neck and have it stay put for a long time. The other neat feature of the cork is that it is permeable to oxygen. This means a low dose of oxygen gets to the wine over the life of its storage. The wine reacts with the oxygen, forming wonderful tertiary flavors and aromas that were not in the wine when it was bottled. We call them tertiary because the primary flavors come from the grape; the secondary flavors are developed in the winery. Things that happen after the winery are tertiary. A few examples would be caramel, cedar, toasted almond, cigar box, and dried leaves.

PRO TIP

Wine aging is just small, controlled amounts of air getting to the wine through the cork.

There is a downside to cork. When the cork is cleaned during production, naturally occurring chemicals in the cork react with the cleaning products to form TCA (2,4,6-trichloroanisole). While this chemical is not harmful to humans, we can detect it into the parts per trillion and it smells like wet dog, musty basement, or wet cardboard. The problem is that sometimes means your wine tastes and smells like one of these undesirable items. Producers have improved their processes, and "corked" wine represents less than 5 percent of all bottles.

PRO TIP

If your wine smells like wet dog or musty basement, it is "corked."

Beyond the positives of aging and the negatives of TCA, there is a romantic element to corks. The visceral feel one has when popping a cork out of a bottle makes you smile. It means good times are ahead, perhaps good food and hopefully time with good friends. This is especially so for that wonderful pop of a Champagne cork.

SCREW CAPS

Screw caps are a relatively perfect closure. Made of aluminum, with a synthetic contact surface with the glass, nothing is getting in or out of the wine with a screw cap. The good news is, no cork means no TCA and no corked wine. The bad news is since there is no oxygen infusion, the wine will not age or change over time. The wine will forever remain the same as when it left the winery.

PRO TIP

Wines with screw caps don't age.

The inert nature of this closure is great for the winemaker since the consumer will drink exactly what they created. Of course, this assumes the wine hasn't been stored on top of the refrigerator or in the trunk of car. Heat will still kill a wine, even with a screw cap.

There are plenty of other closure types, from glass stoppers to synthetic cork to highly engineered polymer and rubber corks. I don't plan to dive into these, but they are all trying to simulate the oxygen permeability of cork without the risk of TCA and hopefully at a lower cost.

Which is better? The answer is that it depends on the wine. For fine wines that deserve to be aged and would benefit from the gentle aging delivered by a cork, a cork is best. This includes many red wines and superior white wines that are designed to be aged to release the full potential of the creation by the winemaker. Simpler reds probably could be in a screw cap because they are "drink now" kinds of wines.

Screw caps can be used for almost all white wines, except a limited number of extremely high-end white wines that develop complexity with age. With simple whites that are designed to be drunk within a year or two of production, a screw cap is perfect. It will retain the fresh fruity character of the wine.

Now, this sounds simple, but there are plenty of simple wines under cork for marketing reasons and for the romantic nature of popping a cork. It makes the wine seem fancy and perhaps more premium than it really is. The other factor is consumer perception. It's hard to conceive of a high-end wine in a screw cap bottle. But if that wine wouldn't benefit from age, like some bottles of Australian shiraz, then a screw cap is fine. The problem is it might not fly off the shelves due to our preconceived views.

Final verdict: Screw cap or cork, there is good wine in either bottle. Drink up!

[22]

THE WINE BUSINESS AT A RESTAURANT

IT'S USEFUL TO UNDERSTAND HOW important the sale of wine and spirits are to the business model of a restaurant—especially Michelin star-caliber restaurants. While the focus might be on the incredible food, high-end ingredients, and top-notch service, a restaurant can only hope to break even. The overhead is too high, the staff too many. That's where alcohol sales come in. They make up the bulk of the profit.

PRO TIP

A high-end restaurant is likely unprofitable without the wine and spirits program.

Part of the way restaurants do that is by marking up bottles of wine. The general rule is that they double to triple the wholesale price of a bottle. In other words, a bottle that might cost them $20 will be listed on the menu for $60. When you are comparing the retail price you will pay at the local wine shop, it will be closer to 2 to 2.5 times. While that might seem high, you need to factor in the cost of buying, inventorying, insuring, labor, cleaning, and replacing glassware as accidents happen. I've been responsible for my fair share of broken glassware, so I should probably pay for a few new glasses. If the mark-up is higher than the range I indicated, they are moving into excessive mark-up territory.

They really can't have these kinds of mark-ups on bottles that retail for $100 and up, so the mark-ups tend to be gentler on more expensive bottles like 1.5 to 2 times rather than 2 to 2.5 times.

PRO TIP

Wine by the bottle averages 2 to 2.5 times the wine store price in the restaurant, less for expensive bottles.

The math is even more dramatic when it comes to pricing wine by the glass. A general rule of portion control is that there should be between four to six glasses of wine in any bottle of wine. The rule that most restaurants follow is that they will price the glass the same as what the bottle cost them at wholesale. If the bottle cost $12 (it will cost you $16–20 at a wine store), then the wine costs $12 by the glass. That means they buy the bottle for $12 and then sell four or five glasses of wine at $12 each, for a total of $48 to $60. That's a remarkable profit!

PRO TIP

Wine by the glass is priced at the wholesale bottle price for a glass.

While wine by the glass might seem expensive, it's actually a great way for you to try something new without the commitment of purchasing an entire bottle—or the guilt at not finishing it if you don't like it. I do this all the time. Many sommeliers, for instance, will express their creativity and style in the kinds of wines available by the glass that are on the menu.

The other factors to consider are inventory and turnover. Only a limited number of wealthy owners can afford a large and deep cellar when many of those wines won't sell for years. The carrying costs can be significant. Usually, there are a limited number of wines that move with great velocity, and even at thinner margins, that can make a lot of money. In a new place or a less well capitalized restaurant, you'll see a small wine list with every wine designed to turn over rapidly.

PRO TIP

On a deep list, many of the wines are consigned by their owners.

One of the secrets of an incredible wine list is that many of those bottles are likely consigned by potentially dozens of private owners. In other words, the owners of that wine put it on the list with the agreement that when the bottle sells in the restaurant, the owner is paid. This is not a path to riches. Sommeliers know the market price of wine so they will pay market or less, even though they sell for wine list prices.

[23]

HOW DOES WINE GET TO YOU?

THE THREE-TIER DISTRIBUTION SYSTEM (MAKER-DISTRIBUTOR-RETAILER) goes back to the repeal of Prohibition in the United States in 1933. The states were put in charge of the laws around distribution of alcohol, but the states and the federal government were mostly concerned about collecting taxes. Most states have outlawed the ownership of the entire chain of distribution to make sure there are clear demarcation points where they can collect taxes, except in some special cases like brewpubs.

Winery or Importer: The production of the product happens here and ends with the cases of wine being placed on a loading dock, at which point the ownership changes to the distributor. The wine is sold quite inexpensively (compared to a wine list price) to the distributors with typical gross margins for a higher end winery being around 50 to 60 percent over costs, according to Silicon Valley Bank. Wineries love to have people come to the estate and buy wine directly, because they make the profit of the entire distribution chain.

Importers are like wineries from the point of view of distribution. They are usually identifying great wines outside the United States and taking the risk to import that wine. They will commit to container loads of wine with the view of selling them to distribution. Most specialize in an area of the world, such as Italy or Australia or Chile. The gross margins of a typical importer are around 30 percent.

Distributor: Because liquor laws vary by state, distributors vary state by state as well, including in some counties that take the role of the distributor and deduct not only the taxes on the wine, but the margin of the distributor. The distributors will commit to producers and importers to take their wine and sell it to restaurants and retailers in their served areas. This creates skilled salespeople with deep wine knowledge and the willingness to provide samples and tasting as part of the sales process. They are also on the hook if a bottle is corked and the retailer returns the bottle and hold a significant amount of inventory in a temperature-controlled warehouse. Typical distributor gross margins are around 30 percent.

Retailer: The bottle finally arrives at the retailer, ready for you to purchase. The retailer has the physical location for your purchase, although over time wine laws are being rationalized and internet marketers are coming into play, like with most markets. Retailers do offer a bunch of valuable services to justify their prices: they hold inventory, have trained staff, light, insure, and maintain temperature for their inventory until you purchase. Typical gross margins are a little higher here at 40 percent, but costs are higher too. There are a few mega-retailers that buy massive quantities at excellent prices and operate on somewhat lower margins, including Total Wine and Costco.

Restaurant: If your wine doesn't go to a retailer, it might go to a restaurant and appear on the wine list. This is the most expensive place to purchase a bottle of wine, but it's a great place to try something new. The normal rule of thumb for a restaurant is to triple their wholesale purchase price to set the wine list price. If they buy it for $30, it might be $90 on the wine list, or a 66 percent gross margin, although some restaurants are little more moderate with their markups. This is designed to cover the staff, storage, training, glassware, and a decent profit. In a prior chapter, I discussed how the wine program can be the reason a great restaurant is profitable. If the bottle is sold by the glass, perhaps at the bar, the rule of thumb is that the glass costs what the bottle does. This assumes six healthy pours per bottle.

Adding It Up: Let's take a bottle of wine that appears on a wine list at $100 and see what everyone in the chain received. The producer made it for $12 to $15 and sold it for $25 to a distributor. They sold it to a restaurant for $35 and the restaurant sold to you for $100. Yes, it seems expensive, but the perfect bottle of wine at the right moment can't be beat.

Part Four
ORDERING ON YOUR OWN IN A RESTAURANT

[24]

THE BEVERAGE SERVICE DANCE

THE BEVERAGE SERVICE IS LIKE a dance between the servers and the people dining at the table. Like all dances, it works best when both parties understand their roles and the timing for an elegant and entertaining waltz.

The Table: When your party arrives at the table, a server will usually place napkins and menus for each diner. If the host is obvious, he or she will be handed the wine list. If it isn't obvious, sometimes the server will ask who will be handling the wine list. Either the host will take the list or ask someone knowledgeable to order for the table.

First Approach: The server then approaches, welcomes everyone to the restaurant, and asks if anyone would like a cocktail. I do like to know the name of the server, and if they don't say it, I will ask. If you are ordering the wine, having someone order a cocktail gives you a bit of welcome time to decipher the list. If you know you want the sommelier to help, now is the time to ask the server to send him or her over. The server might explain any specials from the chef at this point.

Ordering the Wine: For a larger table, I'll usually order at least one white and one red bottle. You'll want to get them both out sooner rather than later as some people don't drink white and will wait for the red. And that way people can have wine as a cocktail if they want. If the server or the sommelier is helping you, they will direct you to some appropriate wines based on your criteria, target price, the menu, and so forth. Ideally, you will have a sense of what people are ordering for food before you order the wine.

Ordering the Food: The server will move around the table, ladies first, taking orders for the elements of the meal. I prefer when they write down the orders, but some servers have excellent memories and can recount the entire table order from their head. As the table enjoys cocktails, they will enter the order and grab the wine to serve.

Presenting and Opening the Wine: I prefer the wine to be presented and poured before the food order is taken as the table can talk and relax with a cocktail or some wine as a cocktail. But sometimes, this happens after the food order is taken and that is acceptable too. The server or sommelier will present the wine, sometimes reading back the label to confirm the order.

PRO TIP

Check the year on the bottle to make sure it is the same as the one in the wine list.

Admittedly, this is a pet peeve of mine as well, but servers switch years of the wine all the time, thinking they are the same. While sometimes that is true, they will swap a superior year for an inferior one. Rarely do you get a better year. I always check and about 30 percent of the time, the wine list wasn't updated, and they are out of the advertised year. You'll have to verify the new year is okay before you take the bottle.

They'll then open the bottle, present the cork, and give a short pour to the host. You are then supposed to taste it and proclaim it acceptable for the table. They'll then pour wine for those that want it.

Pours and Refills: A good wine pour will be four to six ounces, or about 1/4 to 1/3 of the glass. Servers who do giant pours over 1/2 of the glass volume are lazy because they don't want to come back to pour more or they are trying to drive up the wine sales by using up the bottle quickly. A good server will do modest pours and frequently refill as they check the table. They will do the same for water.

Ending the Meal: Sated from a wonderful meal with friends and some nice wine, a good server will ask about dessert and an after-dinner drink. If you have a sweet tooth, it's a great way to end the night. One of the reasons restaurants do this is because the items at the end of the meal have a high margin and drive up the profits of the restaurant. There is a famous restaurant in Tampa, Florida, that has an entire second floor dedicated to the after-entrée portion of the meal and up-selling drinks and desserts.

The Bill: Finally, the bill will be presented to the host. It is usually in a folio so the credit card exchange and payment can be done discretely. When the server is dawdling in bringing the bill, you can always make the universal sign of pretending to scribble on your hand to let them know you are ready. The problem is, this is most appropriate in a New Jersey diner, so when entertaining with clients, you might need to just give "the look," indicating you are done, to the server.

One thing to remember is that in most of Europe, servers are accustomed to people lingering for hours over and after a meal. The servers will not bring the check as that is considered rude. You must ask for it. I've waited a few times for a waiter to read my mind and bring the check until I finally remembered to politely ask.

[25]

WINE-FOOD PAIRING BASICS

AS I'VE MENTIONED IN EARLIER chapters, wine is often best enjoyed with food. I recall a crisp rosé I had with roast chicken at a meal in Paris and the wine and food literally danced across my tongue. The wine and the chicken were good by themselves, but together—magic. Here are some tips you can keep in mind for finding the perfect wine pairing for the dishes you'll be enjoying.

PRO TIP

Match or contrast the intensity and flavors of the food and the wine.

The first tip to consider when pairing a wine is to either match or contrast. This applies to the intensity of the wine and the protein. If you don't match the wine with the food, either one could overwhelm the flavor of the other. If you are having a gently flavored meal like shellfish or lobster, for instance, you might want to pair that with a gently flavored white wine. If you are dining on something more robust like a ribeye steak on the other hand, you'll want to match that with a more intense red wine.

You also need to consider any sauce on the dish when matching or contrasting as well, since that is a major flavor element in the meal. Sometimes you might want to contrast instead of match. If you are going to be having a rich butter sauce, for instance, consider adding some acid from a buttery Chardonnay to balance the meal. If you are eating a stronger flavored pesto-crusted salmon, then you might need a medium-bodied red wine to match the sauce. Moving up to a ribeye with a demi-glace sauce, you'll want a powerful wine to match it and not get overwhelmed. If you have vegetarian friends, then it's usually about pairing with whatever sauce the vegetables are served with, which typically means more subtle flavors than big ones when it comes to your wine. The exception would be when you're eating something with intense flavors like Indian food, where you'll need to find a match for that intensity but contrast the heat of the food.

High-Acid Wines Are Food Friendly: Just like a squeeze of lemon brightens a dish, so does a higher acid wine, so you'll rarely go wrong with a wine that is higher acid. The acid is great at cutting through salty or rich foods, cleansing your palate for the next bite. Select a high-acid wine when having an oily food or a rich cream sauce. The acid in the wine is also mellowed by salt in a dish, so it is a great pairing with something salty. A perfect pairing here is high-acid Champagne and fried chicken, which is both oily and salty.

Salted Foods Are Red Wine Friendly: Salt is easy when it comes to pairing with wine, especially with high-tannin wines like bold reds. The salt in the food softens the tannins and makes the wine more enjoyable. That's the reason a steak and Cabernet Sauvignon go together so well. It isn't the fat in the steak; it's the salt. You can even try putting some salt on your tongue before you take a sip of red wine; it makes it taste mellow and softens the tannins.

Fatty Foods Are Wine Friendly: There's a reason we enjoy wine and cheese: fatty foods make wine taste great. The key is picking a wine that is big and bold with a high acid content. The perfect pairing here is a big Australian Shiraz with a roast lamb loin or spaghetti and meatballs and an Italian Chianti.

Sweet and Spicy Foods Need Sweet Wine: The challenge of pairing wine with something sweet is that you need to go even sweeter when choosing your wine. If you're eating a chocolate tart, for instance, you'll want something very sweet like a Port. Otherwise, the dessert will overwhelm the wine and it will taste like water. Sweet wines are also great for reducing chili heat in a dish, so a slightly sweet Riesling is a great pairing with a spicy Indian or Chinese dish.

Avoid Tannic Wines with Chili Heat and Bitter Foods: Chili heat is the most difficult flavor to pair with because spicy heat will increase any bitterness in the wine, especially from tannins. A good option might be something like a Riesling or Gewürztraminer because they are very low in tannins. But bitter flavors, like broccoli, asparagus, and Brussels sprouts, are also tricky. The problem is that if you pick the wrong wine, you will amplify the metallic bitterness in the food. What you need are wines with low or no tannins, like a Beaujolais, where a little sweetness will offset the bitterness. This is not the time for a high-tannin Napa Cabernet Sauvignon.

PRO TIP

What grows together goes together.

There are an infinite number of good food and wine pairings, but also remember the adage "What grows together, goes together." This is because both the food and wine come from the same terroir and their flavors are influenced by that ground and environment. If I'm eating Spanish food like paella, I'll have Spanish wine with it. And if I am eating Greek, I'll look for an option from there.

Here are some other good pairings that follow these rules:

Grape	Good Pairing
Chardonnay	butter-poached lobster fried chicken (Champagne) root vegetables shellfish

Sauvignon Blanc	goat cheese shellfish white fish, like sole
Riesling	Chinese food Indian food Tex-Mex Vinegar-based salad dressings
Cabernet Sauvignon	steak (aka slab and a cab) game meats (rabbit, boar) short ribs Portobello mushrooms
Pinot Noir	salmon duck game birds (quail, pheasant) pasta
Merlot	pork roast chicken root vegetables
Syrah	game meats dishes with a red sauce BBQ hamburgers

[26]

ORDERING WINE

WHEN YOU LOOK AT MOST wine lists, the selection is organized by bubbles, whites, reds, and after-dinner drinks. Within the white and red sections, the lists are typically built to start with lighter wines, like a Chablis, and bolder, more robust wines toward the end of the section, such as a Napa Cabernet Sauvignon in the red section.

Sometimes the list is organized by geography, where wines from different regions are grouped together. I always appreciate when the list-maker adds the grapes used in the wine, which helps me expand my wine knowledge, even if I don't pick that particular one. It's typical that so-called Old-World wines, grown in countries like France and Italy, don't even list the name of the grape on the label. They only tell you the region the wine is from, which is then supposed to tell you what kind of wine it is.

You can get a view on the quality from the designation of the wine. Consider, for instance, a French wine from Bordeaux or an Italian Chianti. There are also designations these countries include like "Domain Controlled Area" or DOC, which tells you that the grapes in that wine come from one of the better growing regions in the country. Wines like Bordeaux also might include an extra term describing these vineyard designations like first growth or fourth growth, for example, which were mandated by Napoleon for the Exposition Universelle. The designations were assigned on the price of the wine at that time. These things all tend to mean the wine will be of a better quality, and likely more expensive.

All this information can be confusing. It also might not tell you that the wine is really any better than, say, a wine made from American grapes grown in the Napa Valley.

Showing up at a restaurant with clients only to be handed a 100-page wine list can be intimidating. That's why I always go to the restaurant's website ahead of time and spend some time researching their inventory. I will typically choose one or two white wines, as well as two reds. But I'll also have a backup plan in case the wine list online was outdated, or they ran out of a certain selection. When you do your research ahead of time, you can look like a genius in front of people!

PRO TIP

Research the wine list before you go to a restaurant to speed up ordering.

But what happens if you didn't have the time to check ahead of time? When I'm dining with companions, especially a larger group where I don't know what everyone will be eating, I often order Champagne. We just don't drink enough bubbles in our lives! I have even been known to order Champagnes for an entire meal because it truly pairs well with everything. Good Champagne has the depth and complexity to match any food. Other Champagnes of lesser quality, however, are best served with orange juice.

That then begs the next question: How many bottles of wine should you order? The classic measure is that there are six glasses of wine in every bottle, though I do have friends who consider a bottle a single serving! It's reasonable to assume that everyone will have about three glasses of wine across a meal. If there are four of you, that's two bottles. If there are six people, plan on ordering three bottles. You can order them all up front, or you can wait to order bottles based on how people are ordering their food.

Typically, I will start out with an easy-to-drink white wine, like a Chablis, which pairs well with any appetizers people order. After that, if I know there are white wine drinkers at the table, I'll go with something like a Sonoma Chardonnay, a dry Riesling, or even a Sauvignon Blanc from New Zealand. These are all simple, direct, and with high enough acid to pair well with the snacks.

When it comes time to order wine with dinner, I'll go with whites if people are ordering fish and vegetables, or I'll go with reds like Cabernets and Burgundies to pair well with meat. I'll also go to red wines early on if I know I have "red heads" in the group who prefer red to white wine.

Save some money on your wine order by avoiding the popular "branded" wines—names like Caymus, Opus One, Silver Oak—that every sommelier puts on the list to give people the chance to order something with a name they recognize. These wines typically fall lower on the P/Q ratio. They're expensive but don't score that highly on the BLIC scale. You'll typically get a better and more interesting wine by going in a different direction while saving some money. Lots of people love Silver Oak, for instance, but even though they produce more than one million bottles of wine a year, bottles are still $150 a pop. That said, if you are overwhelmed by the wine list, ordering one of these known wines is a smart, low risk ordering strategy. We'll discuss those more in the chapter on low risk ordering strategies.

PRO TIP

Years matter.

When you're ordering wine, recognize that the year of the vintage does matter—often a lot. A single year can make a major difference in quality of a bottle. Usually, lesser bottles of the same maker are priced cheaper, while great years will have a higher price. You can go online to the *Wine Spectator* website and access a chart they have that lists every vintage on the planet. I'll sometimes do this on my phone at the table if I can't recall the quality of a particular year and region. When you order a bottle, take note of the year and bin number on the menu—and then make sure it's the same vintage that's brought to your table.

PRO TIP

Count your corks.

When you're drinking a few bottles of wine, it can be easy to lose track. That's why I keep the corks from the bottles I've ordered. That way, when the check comes, I can make sure I wasn't charged for more than I ordered.

[27]

HOW TO GET THE MOST OUT OF THE WINE LIST

BEING HANDED A WINE LIST at a restaurant can be intimidating, particularly if the list is large and complex. The fancier the restaurant, generally the larger the list. But you can have some fun with a wine list if you know a few pro tips.

The wine list is the creation of the sommelier or perhaps the wine director of the restaurant. Depending on the nature of the restaurant, the approach of the sommelier, and the wine budget, you will see very different lists. Some lists will be encyclopedic and others a bit thin with limited and focused selections. But there are some markers of a good wine list. It will represent the theme of the restaurant, have a range of prices, and feature some reliable standbys, a couple wild cards, and a few epic wines.

PRO TIP

Test the markup.

The first thing I do when I look at a wine list is to find a wine I know well, including the price. I then compare it to the price on the list. You only must do this for one wine to get a feeling for the markup. For example, I am on the mailing list for Williams Seylem wines and buy their 2015 Eastside Neighbors Pinot Noir for $59 a bottle; at retail, it is closer to $80 a bottle. I was recently at a restaurant that had it on the list at $185, or about three times wholesale price and 2.3 times retail price. That is a fair markup since it is between 2 and 2.5 times the retail price, as I discussed in the prior chapter. When the markup is excessive, perhaps closer to three times retail, I tend to order a bit less wine in protest unless I am with clients and cannot do that.

PRO TIP

Drink with the theme.

When you are at a restaurant with an ethnicity, you will be best off drinking wines from that region. There is a reason Italian wines are spectacular with Italian food. They complement and offset each other well, like the way the tight acidity of a chianti cuts through a rich Bolognese sauce.

Look at the type of restaurant and find a wine in your price range from that part of the world and experiment! I go to a fancy Greek restaurant sometimes, and while I rarely drink Greek wines, I do there. And they are fantastic with the food.

PRO TIP

There are prices for all wallets.

On a well-designed wine list, there should be something for every wallet. If you are a college kid out on a fancy date with a new girlfriend or a big-shot executive out to impress clients, the list should have something for you. Know what you want to spend and don't feel bad about ordering it. Sometimes there are gems with an amazing price to quality ratio at the bottom of the list. And sometimes, those big wines with the big reputations don't live up to expectations. Name your price and stick to it.

PRO TIP

Don't forget wine by the glass.

When I first started entertaining in restaurants, the wine by the glass programs were anemic and really didn't feature good wine. This has changed. Now, the wines by the glass are an opportunity to showcase the skill of the sommelier in picking delicious, well-priced wines that work with the food. From my point of view, it's a great way to try a wine I haven't had before without making the commitment to a bottle. If you want a no-strings-attached way to try a wine, grab the by-the-glass menu and try something new. You might find a new wine you love. It's also a great way to moderate how much you are served.

PRO TIP

Stick with old standbys.

Like an old flame, or perhaps a moth to a flame, there are some wines that we keep coming back to because we know they are reliably good and won't disappoint in the glass. That Silver Oak, Alexander Valley Cabernet Sauvignon may not be the world's best wine, but there is a reason it's on a lot of wine lists. It's reasonably priced and delivers decent value for the drinker. You should taste and know two or three popular wines that appear on many wine lists that you like and have them ready to select in a pinch. If nothing jumps off the list at you or you are concerned about picking a bad wine in front of clients, stick to a reliable standby.

PRO TIP

Take the leap for epic wines.

On larger lists, when they have a particularly deep cellar, there will be some epic wines. When I say epic wines, I mean a wine with 30 years of age, from a global class estate, and in a year with perfect growing conditions. These would be wines you might only taste once or twice in a lifetime.

Now clearly, you will want to check the mark-up as we discussed before to determine if they are marking up the wine excessively. But with super high-end wines like this, there is less of a need to get the typical markup so that is a little unlikely. If your budget can swing a monster wine, perhaps for a major celebration or if you have a very generous expense account, it's worth a go. One caution: I would only do this with wine aficionados. If your guests aren't really into wine, save your money and leave the bottle in the cellar for a table that will enjoy it.

I was at an amazing restaurant with some clients and we were having a fancy dinner a few years back. These were all wine people who appreciated good juice. I found a 1982 Château Mouton Rothschild on the list at a bargain price, roughly what I could find it for retail—basically no markup. Now this was not a cheap wine, but it was an amazing value in a restaurant and an epic wine. We all enjoyed it and still talk about that wine and that dinner almost 10 years later. Don't forget to let the sommelier have a little taste when you have an epic wine, and you will have a friend for life.

Use these secrets and have a great time at your next dinner while getting the most out of the wine list.

[28]

HOW MUCH CAN YOU SPEND OF THE HOST'S MONEY?

ONE OF THE MORE UNCOMFORTABLE situations is when you are at a dinner and the host hands you the wine list and asks you to pick. This usually happens when you are the guest of honor—and even more complex, when you're in a foreign country. This is fraught with risk. It's very easy to embarrass yourself or your host with an inappropriate selection. The biggest risk is around selecting a bottle at an unacceptable price.

I have heard of entertaining situations where the host let the client decide on the wine, only to be surprised with a $1,000 bottle of wine, or two, on the bill at the end of the night. That's a tough conversation with your Bud Light-drinking controller when you submit the expense report later that week.

What do you do?

This one is very dependent on your relationship to the host and the level of the people in attendance. If you know the host very well and are comfortable with them, you can ask how much they would like to spend on the bottle. When I do this, I'll usually head over to the host with the wine list and put my finger on a price and ask if they are looking for something like this. If the price is acceptable, they'll agree; and if not, they'll direct me to a different price level—higher or lower.

The other option in this situation is a less formal approach. Just ask the question, "How crazy do you want me to get with the wine?" Sometimes I'll add, "Respectable?" or "Sorry, Bobby, Dad can't afford tuition next semester?" Usually you get some solid direction from the response.

What if the situation is more formal or you don't know the host well?

Target $100 a bottle and adjust from there. There is an expected level of spend for a bottle of wine in a restaurant with a senior audience (think company presidents and business owners). The first rule is $100 a bottle. While that seems high, it does include the restaurant markup and there are usually a few decent bottles within a few dollars of that figure. You'll rarely get chewed out at this price point. If the audience is less senior, scale the price to $75 or even $40 to $50 a bottle. Unless you are given permission, you want to skew on the side of conservative prices.

Target two to three times the average entrée. There is another gauge that I'll use and that is two to three times the average entrée price. If I am in a fancy steak house where the average entrée is $50 to $60 a plate, I don't feel bad about selecting a $150 bottle of wine. If I am told to go crazy, I can double this figure to $200 to $300 a bottle. Anything above those already high figures really demands you talk with the host for agreement before you order. You don't want that uncomfortable moment when the host gets the bill and glares at you across the table for your exorbitant spending on wine.

Gauge your audience when picking a target price. The other factor I consider is the wine knowledge of the audience. If we have a bunch of novices around the table out for a good time, there is no need to go crazy. Typically, $50 a bottle is plenty. If I have a bunch of snooty wine aficionados, we might head more toward the crazy or crazy-plus side of the wine list.

When in doubt, pick a "lifesaver" wine. There are a few wines placed on wine lists that play the role of the "businessperson's lifesaver." In other words, they aren't too expensive and represent decent quality and brands that people know. They'll never get upset at ordering something like Silver Oak, Caymus, or Jordan. If I don't want one of these volume producers, I'll use the price on the list as a guide to find something else. If the Silver Oak Alexander Valley is $125 a bottle, that is my target for the bottle I select. If I am lazy, I just go for the Silver Oak. I know I beat these wines up earlier, but they are good, safe choices in a pinch.

Split the wine and the meal. The other strategy I have employed from time to time is to ask my host to buy the dinner and I'll pick up the wine. This avoids any embarrassment of worrying about prices. It also becomes a nice way to split the bill, and I can order whatever wine looks most interesting to me—everybody wins!

PRO TIP

Price selection is the duty of the host.

This chapter was all about the stress and the strategy when the host hands you the wine list and you must discern the target price on your own. The pro move for a host is to hand the list over and suggest a price range. Saying something like "Jim, why don't you try to find us something fun around $100 a bottle" saves a lot of stress and guessing and potential embarrassment.

Ideally, when you ask how crazy the host wants to get, they respond with "I want to regret I ever handed you that list when I get the bill!" That's time to ask for the reserve wine list.

[29]

LOW-RISK ORDERING STRATEGIES

IT CAN BE IMPOSING TO be handed a wine list and needing to decide quickly. When you are pressed for time and really can't study the list, you need some go-to strategies on how to order.

Here are a few low risk ordering strategies for you to try the next time you need to pull a rabbit out of a hat, or a bottle of wine off a list.

Your Server: While I am not normally a fan of asking the server for a wine recommendation, due to the spotty levels of training unless you are in a top restaurant, this is an option. Often, they will pick something on special or a wine that they happen to sell a lot of. I can tell you from personal experience I always recommended Mouton-Cadet, a moderately priced volume Bordeaux as my go-to wine when I waited tables in college—and knew nothing about wine. In a pinch, though, the server recommendation is likely to be a modestly priced inoffensive choice.

The Sommelier: If you are dining in a fancier place, they are likely to have a sommelier or perhaps a general manager who acts as the sommelier. Talking to them is a solid choice, although a little bit riskier if it is the general manager. They will know the list, know the food, and be able to pick a solid bottle, particularly if you use one of the professional drinking techniques to communicate your price point.

Featured Wines: Some wine lists have a page of featured wines. They are usually labeled "Our Favorites" or "Sommelier Choices." These can be good low-risk selections as they have been vetted by the management and designed to match the menu. You'll have to be aware of what people have ordered and not get a light white when people are going for heavily sauced proteins, or a massive red wine when the table is eating delicate white fish. If the table is large enough, getting a bottle of white and a bottle of red from the featured list is a solid approach.

Wines by the Glass: If there isn't a featured bottle section, the restaurant will almost always have a wine-by-the-glass section on the drink menu. These are the down-the-middle wines that they move in volume. They will always have a by-the-bottle price too, which is where you are going. Some people turn their noses up at wines by the glass, but the reason they move is because they are well priced and tasty. It's hard to go too far wrong here. It is unlikely that you'll have a "wow" moment, but they are serviceable, good choices that won't get you in trouble.

Recommended Pairings: Many times, there will be a wine recommendation on the menu alongside the featured dishes to make things easy for diners (and sometimes to move some excess wine). An example might be for the grilled dover sole, for which they would recommend a French Chablis or a Sonoma chardonnay, both bottles on the wine list. While this can feel like cheating, it's a known good combination. The chef and the sommelier got together to talk through the dish and pick a great wine to pair it. You can certainly go on your own, but if these experts are recommending something, it behooves you to pay attention. When you take this approach, you'll need to be aware of what people are eating and select a white and a red that matches the meals. The good news is that they limited your choices to a very small set of good options.

If you feel like you have the knowledge or the confidence, or both, to dive into the wine list and make selections, have at it. For me, that's part of the fun of going to a new restaurant. If you don't, try one of these easy approaches.

[30]

WINE LIST VALUE PLAYS

THE WINE LIST CAN BE intimidating, especially when you are on a budget. While it's easy to step up to the plate and order a $200 bottle to get a good wine, there are plenty of choices on a wine list where you can have an awesome bottle of wine and not break the bank.

Here are a few of my favorite wine styles that give lots of quality for the price.

BEAUJOLAIS

One of my favorite places to look for value is for a nice Beaujolais. This is an area that grows wine in France and lies just south of the super-expensive and renowned (for good reason) Burgundy. They primarily grow the gamay grape in this area, which has a thicker skin and lower tannins. Wine has been grown in this area back to the Roman times. Funny enough, they used to grow gamay in Burgundy, but a few different noblemen preferred Pinot Noir and so those vineyards were replanted. I guess they never made it all the way south to Beaujolais.

There are four levels of quality that you should be aware of in this area. The first three are not really of a quality for a business meal unless it is super casual.

Beaujolais Nouveau, or Beaujolais Appellation d'Origine Contrôlée (AOC), are very inexpensive and simple wines. Great for sipping in your backyard but not over dinner. Beaujolais Villages is the third highest level, and these wines come from a narrower portion of the defined AOC with better growing conditions, but usually still not what you want for guests.

Beaujolais Cru is the highest level of production and this is where you should go for that bottle off the wine list. These are grown in 10 villages in the Beaujolais area with the best growing conditions, like slate ground and southern exposure for the slopes. At their best, they will remind you of a Burgundy, although they tend to be a little less serious and more approachable wine. Sometimes, you won't see Beaujolais on the label and only the name of the Cru, but on a wine list it will be in the Beaujolais section.

Three of my favorites in this area are Fleurie, Moulin-A-Vent, and Morgon. Fleurie means flower in French, and these wines tend to be more aromatic and pretty when you drink them. The second two are weightier and approach the flavors of a Burgundy, especially Morgon. You should expect to pay $50 to $80 for a nice bottle of Beaujolais, which compares to the high $100 to $200 for a Burgundy.

As for pairing, I find a higher-end Beaujolais is a food-friendly wine with nice tart strawberry fruit and a bit of tannin for structure. That means it can pair elegantly with anything from a sauced fish to a ribeye.

RIESLING

"All Rieslings are sweet and yuck! Perhaps double yuck. And don't you know sugar kills?" That's how a lot of people feel about Rieslings, and fortunately for the rest of us, they are dead wrong. Rieslings are made in a range of sweetness from bone dry to a luscious dessert in a glass. I suppose that the preconceived notion that this elegant wine is always sweet is the reason it is out of favor and following the general and unfortunate downward slide of sweeter wines.

Germany is the King of Riesling. The grape loves the cooler climate and the sloped slate vineyards. Unfortunately, this cooler climate means they are always in pursuit of ripeness, which is to say sugar, in the grapes used to produce the wine. Some of the best areas are Mosel, Rheingau, and Nahe. The Germans have been growing this grape and making wine for more than 500 years, so they have the hang of it. But excellent and bone-dry wines with this grape are also made in France in Alsace, Austria, the Finger Lakes of the USA, Australia in Clare Valley, and some other areas.

Dry Rieslings feature wonderful stone fruit and tropical fruits as well as floral notes with a crisp acidity that many of us are seeking in our white wine. They go well with medium-weight white proteins as well as lighter sauces. Having said that, I could see drinking one throughout a meal and being very happy.

When selecting a German Riesling, stick with the areas I indicated above and go for a Kabinett or a Troken-style wine, which are the driest styles made in Germany. One of the things people confuse in good dry Riesling is the very little sugar in the wine versus the ripeness of the fruit on the nose and the palate. There also quality dry Rieslings from France, Australia, and Austria.

SPANISH RIOJA

Spanish wines currently offer excellent values and they typically pair well with food. The grapes are grown in some fabulous areas and then aged in American oak over many years—which is incredibly expensive. And yet you can get a Grand Reserve Rioja, which has been aged for up to seven years, for between $50 and $60—and it's ready to drink now.

There are Riojas that have not been aged as much as a Grand Riserva that can present great values. The youngest, Crianza, and the moderately aged Riserva are similar wines without the extended aging requirements in the bodega and are great choices. Unlike

Beaujolais, you can go for these lesser designations and get a nice wine for the price.

MAGNUMS: SIZE MATTERS!

One of the value plays you might be missing on the wine list is magnums, those large-format (and slightly intimidating) bottles. They look great on display and clearly say that some group had a great time! But they can be a great value on the wine list too.

A normal bottle of wine is 750 milliliters, or a little less than a quart. There is a debate as to why that has become the standard size. One theory is that it is exactly six services of 125 milliliters, typically served in an osteria in Italy. Another group claims it goes back to the 18th century when they started storing wine in bottles and the largest practical bottle of the time was 750 milliliters. Those theories aside, the EU declared 750 milliliters the standard bottle size in 1975.

While 750 milliliters is the standard, there are larger formats, all on multiples of the basic 750-milliliter bottle. Magnums are 1,500 milliliters (1.5 liters), and double magnums are 3,000 milliliters (3.0 liters)—and they go up from there!

Not all restaurants have magnum-sized bottles, but those with a deep wine list will normally have a smaller selection of better wines in this size (and sometimes larger). The good news about magnums is that the wine generally ages a bit slower, so older vintages can still be fresh and delicious. The downside is that magnums don't turn as fast as normal 750-milliliter bottles. That's part of the reason for a smaller selection.

But this slow turn of older wines presents a golden opportunity for us wine consumers: Magnums aren't generally priced at twice the cost of a similar bottle. Now, this isn't always true. For top-level wines, they have added the marketing premium for the special nature of a magnum, and you may find a magnum is more expensive than two regular bottles. You'll have to look down the list a little to up-and-coming regions as well as third and fourth growths.

Let's start with the obvious—you need a decent-size group to polish off a magnum. Even at the typical pour of six glasses to a bottle, you'll have 12 glasses to work with. My experience is that six people is the minimum needed to buy a magnum. Your nice purchase isn't so cheap when you leave a bunch of wine in the bottle. But if your group can get through a magnum, it's potentially a great value against buying by the bottle.

[31]

WHAT IF YOUR BUSINESS DINING PARTNER DOESN'T DRINK?

WHILE DRINKING DOESN'T HAVE THE stigma of smoking in public, there is a camp of people who for personal or religious reasons choose not to drink. That's not a problem; it just means more for those who do, or perhaps a better bottle of wine with fewer people enjoying!

How do you handle it when you don't know your partner's view on drinking, and you are headed to a place with creative cocktails and a wonderful wine list? Even further, how do you handle it if you know they don't drink?

Grace is the first word that comes to mind in this situation, and it must go both ways. Hopefully, you have the grace to not imbibe if your partner would truly not appreciate it. On the other side, if you do choose to have an adult beverage, they will hopefully have the grace to not be offended, although you might get a look.

The strategy here is different for a smaller group, perhaps two to four diners versus a larger group. In a smaller group, I'll ask if my partner will be having a cocktail or if they'd like to have some wine with dinner. If they are open, then feel free to order, matching your consumption with theirs. If they are a one and done drinker, you can go one more than them, but no more. If they are a heavy drinker, feel free to tap the brakes whenever you want. If you are a heavy drinker and they aren't, you can hit the bar after dinner.

PRO TIP

You can have one drink more than your dinner partner.

If my dining partner doesn't drink, I'll usually ask if it is due to religious or personal reasons. Mostly because I am curious, and it has led to some interesting conversations about their life or their religion. You have to pick your spot on asking this question, particularly your comfort with your dining companion and how formal they are. In a highly formal setting with a stiffer person, I'd keep my conversation to the weather and away from personal drinking choices. If there are just two at the meal, then I wouldn't drink. If there are four, it is possible to ask if they mind if you do, but preferably you don't want to be the only one with a drink. Most businesspeople who choose not to drink have been in this situation many times and it is usually not an issue to proceed, but it is polite to ask their permission.

In a larger group, if a few people are imbibing, then it is perfectly okay for a few to pass. I generally wouldn't ask why someone passes on a cocktail in a larger group at the risk of offending or embarrassing them. That move only works in a more intimate setting.

There are many reasons people choose not to drink, perhaps a family issue, health concerns, addiction, or just an early morning and a desire to be fresh. There are a few religious groups that you might do business with that do not drink. Be respectful and just plan on not drinking unless invited to do so.

[32]

HOW TO BRING A BOTTLE OF WINE TO A RESTAURANT

WE ALL HAVE A FEW favorite restaurants that deliver amazing service, great food, and...an uninspiring wine list. Fortunately, there is an alternative to forcing yourself to drink something you don't want. This is an ideal time to bring that special bottle of wine, or two, from your cellar along with you. But how do you do it?

As I've mentioned, restaurants make a lot of their profit with their alcohol sales. This isn't surprising as a high-end restaurant will normally make 30 to 50 percent of their revenue from wine and spirits, and the markups are quite large. Even many two- and three-star Michelin restaurants, which are renowned for their food, would probably operate in the red if it weren't for their robust wine programs. That means that since we are taking the opportunity to make money off our wine selections out of the restaurant's hands, we need to tread carefully.

The first order of business is to check their wine list. You can typically do this online since many restaurants will put their wine menu on their website for your advance study. If they have the same bottle as you intend to bring, then it's a non-starter: you can't do it. Now, if they have the same brand of Italian wine in a 2012 vintage, but you have bottle from 1996—that technically isn't the same bottle. Most restaurants need to rotate their wine inventory, and this makes it hard to hold onto older bottles like that unless they have a very large inventory, which means you're in the clear.

The second polite thing to do is to call the restaurant and ask what their policy is regarding bringing wine to dinner. Usually, they are happy to let you know. A typical arrangement would be a maximum of two outside bottles for a table of four, with the bonus that you can bring an extra one for every bottle you buy off the list. I'll typically also ask if the wine list on the website is accurate. It would be embarrassing to bring a bottle just to find they changed their list and have exactly your bottle available. And they'd be happy to sell it to you for three times what you paid, too!

When you arrive, you'll want to hand the bottles over to the wine steward or sommelier. They are still going to provide the service of chilling, opening, providing glassware, and serving the wine as though you purchased it. This doesn't come for free, however. You will usually pay a corkage fee for the wine service that ranges from $10 up to $50 per bottle in a high-end restaurant (even higher if you're in a major city like New York). That means you will want to make sure you are bringing a bottle that is worth that kind of service fee; your bottle of "Two Buck Chuck" just isn't going to be cost efficient.

At this point, it's just like you purchased the bottle. The service and pacing should be exactly as you would expect. Frankly, since you are paying for it with the corkage, it should be!

One trick that insiders use is to offer a taste to the sommelier if you have brought a particularly special bottle. I'll usually ask if they have ever tasted this wine. If not, I'll tell them to please take some if they'd like. Sommeliers are wine geeks and they live to taste new and special bottles. If you really reached deep into your cellar, you'll make their night. And sometimes, the corkage fee will magically disappear from your bill!

PRO TIP

Tip accordingly no matter the bill.

There are times when you'll find that the corkage fee is missing from the bill when you've brought a bottle of wine to the restaurant. This was probably intentional. Regardless, tip accordingly as if that charge were there. It's the right thing to do.

Don't be intimidated when it comes to bringing your own bottles of wine to a restaurant. Just do your research, be respectful of the process, and be sure to tip your sommelier.

[33]

THE BITTER SECRET ABOUT SWEET WINES

ONE OF THE MOST MISUSED words when people order wine is "sweet." When seasoned wine people say a wine is sweet, they mean that there is residual sugar in the wine; in other words, not all the grape juice has been converted into alcohol. This is a winemaker choice. When a diner asks for sweet wine, many times they mean fruity, with lots of juicy fruit on the nose and palate.

PRO TIP

Tell your server if you want fruity wine or a wine with sugar.

But there is a lot more to sweet wines. When grapes are grown for winemaking, the grower will try to generate as much sugar in the grape as possible. They do this through plot selection, how long they let the grapes stay on the vine, when they pick them, and mostly lots of praying for good weather. The level of sugar, measured in a unit called brix, controls the upper limit for most premium wines (some winemakers will add a little sugar later in the process).

In typical wine production, the yeast eats all that delicious sugar and creates alcohol and CO_2. The winemaker usually lets that yeast go until all the sugar is consumed, and that creates a relatively dry-style wine. That's the most common style of wine. As I indicated above, they can be juicy and fruity and seem sweet, but if one were to measure how much residual sugar was in the wine, it wouldn't be much—although almost all wines have a little sugar left in them, even Brut Champagne.

When the winemaker is specifically going for a sweet wine, they can stop the yeast from consuming all the sugar using a few techniques like chilling the wine or filtering off the yeast. That leaves a wine with a controlled amount of alcohol and some grape sugar in the wine. You get the best of both worlds: alcohol and a nice fresh fruit flavor with a bit of sugar. It's important to realize that since we start with a known amount of grape juice sugar, if we want a little left in the wine, the alcohol is going to be a little lower. Some very sweet wines might have alcohol content as low as 5 percent.

If the style the winemaker is going for is cloyingly sweet, they must change how they harvest the grapes to have highly concentrated sugar, beyond that in a normal harvest. There are a few ways to do this, but two popular ones are to allow a mold to grow on the outside of the grape. Yes, it sounds gross, but botrytis is a mold that naturally occurs and is used to make the sweetest German Rieslings and the delicious French Sauternes. The mold sucks the water out of the grapes, basically turning them into raisins. Winemakers press these raisins to get a super sugary grape juice that turns into the ultimate high-sugar, low-alcohol wines.

Another technique is to leave the grapes on the vine far past a normal harvest date into the winter, until they freeze on the vine. This is used in some German wines and Rieslings from upstate New York and Canada. You'll know them as Ice-wine (or Eiswein). The frozen grapes are pressed immediately as the freezing captures a lot of the water in the form of ice and the grape juice that flows is very high sugar, just like our raisins in the above example. The wine that is then produced has a similar high-sugar, low-alcohol profile, but with a bright fruitiness.

It's probably no surprise that both approaches are expensive. Hoping for mold or freezing grapes and then making wine from the little dribbles of super-sweet grape juice is not a low-cost approach. When you are thinking about drinking one, try to keep in mind how much went into the final product. It's probably a value choice when you add it up.

Most sweet wines, such as Port, Sauternes, Moscato, and Madeira, are considered dessert wines. I have to say, after a big meal, many times I'll opt for a nice dessert wine to end things. They have that sweetness you crave and without much alcohol. This is a great area to purchase by the glass to avoid the big prices on a bottle of these expensive wines (unless you have a lot of friends joining you at dinner).

There are several inexpensive wines that are sweet by design, or manufacture. People have a sweet tooth, and this goes back to our caveman days, because sweet things were dense in the calories we needed to survive. Manufacturers of volume wines know this, and they will add additional sugar to the wines to make them tasty and accessible. Higher end wines will normally stick only to the natural sugars in the grapes (with a few exceptions).

PRO TIP

Here's the dirty little secret: Most sweet wines usually don't have any more calories than dry wines on a volume basis.

Even better, we normally have smaller servings of sweet wines. Alcohol has around eight calories per gram and sugar has around four calories per gram, which means when we convert two sugars into one alcohol, it's an even calorie trade. If you are avoiding sweet wines because of calories, you can jump in and indulge. If you are a super-paleo Cross-Fitter avoiding sugar, you need to skip the alcohol too (and what fun is that?).

Here's a look at the calorie counts of nine of the most popular sweet wines, from least to most (four-ounce pours, unless noted):

Wine	**Glass**	**Bottle**
German Spatlese Riesling	73	333
French Cabernet Sauvignon	106	480
German Auslese Riesling	106	480
Napa Cabernet Sauvignon	115	520
California Zinfandel	125	564
Australian Shiraz	126	570
French Sauterne (2 oz. glass)	90	810
Ruby Port (2 oz. glass)	103	929
Tawny Port (2 oz. glass)	106	950

Source: Wine Folly

The next time you are considering dessert, pick a sweet wine instead. You can enjoy this delicious style of wine guilt-free, knowing that you are consuming fewer calories than your friend with the pie à la mode.

[34]

HOW ABOUT A PORT AFTER DINNER?

AFTER A WONDERFUL MEAL WITH clients, rather than dessert some people opt for Port. It's a great way to let the meal settle and relax and talk. But what is Port and what are the differences between ruby, tawny, and vintage?

Generically, Port is a red, fortified wine from the Douro region of Portugal. It is sweet and rich, which makes it perfect for something to replace dessert after a meal. I usually order by the glass, because even a table likely won't finish a full bottle.

Originally, Port was developed to create a product that could be stored for a long time and shipped to other countries. The fortification in the wine allows for this. Port became an important element of trade between Portugal and England, where it was and remains a popular beverage. The name came from the city of Porto as the primary shipping location for Port to customers around the world.

The wine is made from red grapes using traditional growing, harvesting, and winemaking methods. Port becomes special when the fermentation is stopped with the addition of a neutral grape spirit known as aguardiente. This leaves a fair amount of residual sugar in the basic wine and increases the alcohol content, which acts as a preservative. Once the fermentation is stopped, the Port is stored in barrels to oxidize it and give flavor, with the level of oxidation changing with the style.

There are many kinds of Port including rosé and white, but most Ports fall into three categories:

Ruby (Red) Port: a deeply colored red Port Vintage that has no year designation. Ruby Port is the least expensive and most popular type of Port. After the fermentation process, the wine is stored in concrete or stainless-steel barrels, which prevents the oxidative aging that typifies Tawny Port and retains the ruby red color. Once the wine is filtered, it is bottled and sent to market. These relatively simple Ports don't benefit from age.

Tawny Port: a very sweet barrel-aged Port with oxidative nut and caramel flavors. Tawny Port is aged a long time in the barrel, which mellows the drink to a golden-brown color. The extensive exposure to oxygen gives a nutty flavor. They are blended across multiple vintages to give the distinctive house style, much like non-vintage Champagnes. The age indicated on a Tawny Port represents the age profile of the wine as they are blended, not a minimum.

Vintage Port: Vintage Ports are made in the same manner as Ruby Ports, but like vintage Champagne, they are not made every year. You'll recognize a Vintage Port because it will have a specific year on the label. The Port houses decide individually if a year is exceptional enough to make a single vintage Port. They take this decision seriously as their reputation for quality is at stake. It generally happens around three times a decade.

Once the wine is fermented, it spends a maximum of two and half years in a cask or in stainless steel, while retaining the fruit and deep red color. The wine is then bottled and aged in the bottle. The bottle aging can last a long time—usually 10 to 40 years before release to the market.

The good news is that the use of exceptional grapes in good years and this extended winemaking process creates wines that are age worthy. It is not uncommon to see bottles of Port for sale at auction that date back to the 1800s that are drinking well.

The next time you consider something sweet after dinner, try a Port—you won't be disappointed. They also make a unique gift to a special client.

[35]

WOMEN AND PROFESSIONAL DRINKING

LET ME START WITH HOW much of a stretch this is for me as a man to write. But I have interviewed several female associates and CEO clients to gain some insight. There are a few guidelines they shared that are worth noting. I want to be clear that I am not perpetuating some of these situations, but simply trying to inform so women in a business situation can make good, heads-up decisions.

NEVER DRINK TOO MUCH IN A BUSINESS SITUATION.

Yes, that's true for the men as well, but unfortunately repercussions for women that cross this one can be more severe. It's just too easy to end up in a bad situation and impact your business or personal reputation with a few drinks on board. Have fun, hang with the team—just manage your consumption. No, it isn't fair, and yes, it is better than it was years ago, but you'd give the same advice to your daughter.

YOU AREN'T GETTING HANDED THE WINE LIST.

I asked Lynn Murphy, CEO of Startech, what women leaders do when handed the wine list. She laughed at me. Neither waiters nor your dining companions will hand you the wine list, even if you are paying—and that's a sad situation. Most women have developed a way of non-verbally communicating to the server that they are paying, and you should hand the list to me if you want a decent tip! The other move is to be known as the wine person at the table and people will naturally hand you the list to get a good pick (because most people don't know how to order, hence this book). The final strategy is to ask the table who knows wine and give them an opportunity to peruse the list, delegating the task. It maintains a control position if you are the boss, but everyone can have the best experience. My friend Linda Rabbit, a successful construction industry CEO, has a more direct approach. When the waiter doesn't hand her the list, she yells over, "Want a tip? Here's a tip: You better give me the wine list!"

YOU CAN'T DRINK AS MUCH AS THE MEN.

This one isn't a universal verity, but most women are simply not as physically heavy as the men. On that basis alone, they take less alcohol to become inebriated. Men have been taking advantage of this for years, telling the woman they must match drink for drink. The smart woman doesn't take the bait—this is the very definition of bringing a knife to a gun fight, to paraphrase Sean Connery in *The Untouchables.* There are exceptions of women who can match the men, and this is a superpower because no man expects it. Use the force for good.

LEAVE THE PARTY EARLY.

As I mentioned earlier in the book, no good decisions get made after 11 p.m. Drinks, fine. Dinner, fine. After-dinner drink, one and done. Frankly, the guys should head to bed after one after-dinner drink too, so this advice isn't different for them. Julie Walker, CEO of 479 Retail, said that this simple idea kept her reputation solid when working in a male-dominated industry.

Those genius business ideas scribbled on a soggy cocktail napkin after too many drinks don't make any sense at breakfast anyway. On a related note, if you are at an event and headed to your room, it's ideal to head out with a very trusted friend, preferably female, just to avoid any made-up gossip, according to Julie.

HAVE A COCKTAIL YOU LIKE.

One of the ways people measure each other when professionally drinking is their choice of cocktail. Yes, it's not fair, but it's the truth. There are two choices on how to go here. The first is to have a signature cocktail and it can be as feminine as you want. I have a friend who is a very popular public speaker and she orders Champagne—always—and if you've ever met Neen, it's brand consistent. And I had a male client who ordered margaritas no matter where he went—it was his drink. It was kind of a party drink so arguably not a business cocktail, but it was his. So, make a Pink Lady, Cosmo, or Appletini yours! The other approach is to have a drink that signals more masculinity, like a martini or even a Manhattan. It lets the guys know that you don't take any guff.

This is a delicate topic and most of the advice is similar to what you would give to a young mentee. But a few areas deserve special focus for a woman to be a skilled professional drinker.

Part Five
DRINKING WINE LIKE A PROFESSIONAL

[36]

WHAT DO YOU DO WITH THE CORK?

IMAGINE THAT YOU'RE OUT TO dinner with clients. You've taken them to a nice place, the kind of restaurant that employs a sommelier to help you with your wine selection. It's high class all the way, and you know you're going to get something delicious no matter what. Then the moment of truth arrives: The sommelier opens your bottle for you and then hands you the cork cradled inside a serviette.

While that's all well and nice, what the heck are you supposed to do with that cork? Your cheeks probably flush knowing that your clients, let alone the sommelier, are staring at you to see what you do. How do you not embarrass yourself? Do you smell it, feel it, lick it, or what?

It turns out there is a simple answer for handling a newly opened cork. But let me first share a little history for context.

Wine has been around as long as man has had access to grapes. But it wasn't until the 1800s that vintners began using corks as stoppers for wine. Prior to that, most vintners would use rags instead. One of the reasons that corks became popular was that they gave winemakers the ability to mark the name of the wine and the year it was made at a time when counterfeiting was quite prevalent. While it was easy to switch the paper label someone might glue to a bottle (the adhesives weren't that good back then), branding the cork was an effective way to ensure you were buying and drinking what you had purchased.

New technology has led to alternatives to corks in more recent years, such as plastic or synthetic corks and even screw tops. They have an advantage in that when you use natural cork, there is the potential threat of contaminating the wine with something called TCA. I'll get into that more shortly.

But about 60 percent of the 20 billion bottles of wine that are produced each year still use cork stoppers. There is still nothing like that visceral feeling of levering a cork out of a tasty bottle of wine. Pop!

That's all great, but what the heck are we supposed to do with it when someone hands us one at dinner?

The most common answer I get when I ask my dinner companions what they think they should do is to smell it. While that might seem reasonable, it's not the correct answer. In fact, if you see someone taking a big whiff of a newly popped cork, you might feel a little embarrassed for them—as was the case recently when a waiter at a fancy restaurant made a big show of sniffing my cork for me like it was a newly found truffle!

When someone hands you a cork, the right response is to first read the cork to make sure it's the same vintage that you selected. Even though a good sommelier will have already pointed out the estate and year before they open it, it can't hurt to check, right?

PRO TIP

Check the maker and vintage on the cork.

The other thing you can do is to feel the tip of the cork. If wine has been properly stored, just the tip should be somewhat moist and pliant and, if it's a red wine, stained red as well. If your cork is dry—or, worse, crumbly—then you have a serious red flag. There is one other thing to look for: if the wine has leaked up along the cork, staining it, which means there wasn't a good seal, and the wine may be oxidized.

PRO TIP

Make sure the cork is not crumbly and the wine hasn't leaked.

One key advantage of natural cork is that it allows oxygen to interact with the wine at a very slow rate, which allows the wine to age gradually over time. But the drier a cork is, the more oxygen it allows into the wine—which ages it faster than the vintner intended. If your cork is dry enough that it crumbles to your touch, you will want to immediately point that out to your sommelier or waiter, as it is a sure sign that something has gone wrong with your wine. The same goes for if the wine has leaked along the cork, allowing excess oxygen in.

The next time you're out to a special meal, don't sweat it when the time comes to uncork your wine. Act like a pro: Give a quick glance at the labeling and then a little squeeze—without ever putting it near your nose.

[37]

WHAT DO YOU DO WHEN YOU TASTE THE WINE?

ONE OF THE MOST STRESSFUL elements of the wine service dance is the tasting of the wine. As the host, all eyes are on you as the waiter stands, bottle poised to serve, and you are supposed to declare the bottle acceptable. But what are you really supposed to be tasting for? If the wine is well balanced? Too tart? Just right?

What you are supposed to do is quite simple in theory and a little hard to do in practice. The primary thing you are doing is tasting to make sure the wine is acceptable for your guests and specifically if the wine is flawed. Now, you don't have to analyze if the tannins are in balance or if the winemaker had a heavy hand with the oak. You are simply tasting to see if there is a wet dog in your glass.

The primary flaw you are looking for is if the wine is "corked." This happens only in bottles with corks, so if your wine has a screw cap, you have no worries. The reason a bottle becomes corked is a chemical known as TCA (trichloroanisole), which is a compound that forms when a mold in the cork reacts with the cleaning agents used in the production of the cork. With modern techniques, this happens in about 2 to 5 percent of bottles of wine with corks, or about a bottle every two cases. Odds are we have all had a glass of corked wine or two in our day. It can sometimes be subtle and not enough to be unacceptable.

When you smell the wine, you will smell wet dog, wet card-board, or wet basement. It is a musty, dank smell that is a little off-putting. This is different than the earthy barnyard scent you pick up in Old World reds. Some corked wines will present obvious musty notes and others are a little subtle and possibly drinkable, although you shouldn't, because life is too short to drink bad wine. I will usually taste a corked wine to be sure it has that same mustiness on the palate—my sacrifice for my friends at the table!

If you think a wine is corked, you should comment gently to the sommelier that you think the wine might be corked and invite them to taste. Here is where their training comes in. In an excellent restaurant, they will whisk away the bottle and taste it in private, perhaps with another sommelier. They will not object to your analysis.

If the wine is in fact corked, they will offer another bottle of the same or an alternative similar bottle. You shouldn't have any fear in taking another of the same as TCA can vary from bottle to bottle, and a single bottle in a case can be corked and the rest can be just fine.

When the new bottle comes to the table, the sommelier will usually offer to taste the wine to ensure this second bottle is not corked. Let them do it, as they are your partner in getting an acceptable bottle to your guests.

Additionally, make sure they replace your glass since the original glass is now contaminated with TCA that can only be removed with cleaning. If your table carries on to a second or third bottle, you should taste each of those before pouring as well. TCA varies by bottle, so just because one was acceptable, the next one could be okay or not—it is random.

PRO TIP

No one gets hurt if you send back a bottle.

You should never be embarrassed about declaring a wine corked, and there is no reason to suffer through a bad bottle. The restaurant won't be offended since they didn't make the bottle. Even better, they will not be economically hurt. If the bottle is truly corked, they will return the bottle to the distributor for a refund, as this flaw is part of the wine business and there is an anticipated rate of return.

If the wine is not corked in their analysis, they will sell the bottle by the glass from the bar. This way, they can move the unused wine and frankly, make more money on the bottle. Don't worry about declaring a wine corked—the restaurant will be just fine.

In a bad restaurant, the sommelier will fight your analysis and declare the wine acceptable if they find it without flaw. Stick to your guns. This is all about your pleasure and the pleasure of your guests. Insist on a replacement or an alternate bottle. If the sommelier is unreasonable, escalate to the manager of the restaurant, and they will almost certainly make it right for you.

Next time you are offered to taste the wine, swirl, smell, and taste. If there isn't a musty wet dog in the glass, declare it acceptable and have the sommelier pour for the table.

[38]

HOW TO SMELL YOUR WINE

WHEN HOLLYWOOD PORTRAYS A WINE connoisseur, they are swirling their wine, dipping their noses into the glass, and taking a big whiff. It's iconic. But is this the right way? How do the experts smell their wine?

Glassware is the first thing that matters for the olfactory appreciation of the wine. Different wines have different aromas and require different glasses to properly enjoy them, whether it's a narrow top to contain the delicate aromas or a larger bowl to allow a powerful wine to breathe. I recently had a nice French sparkling wine poured into a wide-top glass. By the time I drank it, it wasn't so sparkling. If you have the right glass, use it. If not, a generic red wine glass can do for most needs.

The second element of enjoying the wine is a proper pour in the glass. Generally, this is 25 to 33 percent of the volume of the glass. This means there is plenty of headspace for the smells to release and concentrate and gives you a space for your nose without getting your beak wet. Don't worry if it seems like a short pour—the somm will give you more. Beyond the accumulating of the odors, it is hard to swirl a glass that is 70 percent full without sending some over the edge.

Over time, I have practiced smelling the wines I drink, before pouring back an ample swig. It turns out you can learn to smell what is in the glass. In my opinion, it is more about lacking the vocabulary to describe what your nose is picking up. There has been some research that indicates the human nose can discern up to one trillion different scents. While this seems optimistically high, even if they were off by a factor of a million—we could still smell one million different scents. The problem is the Oxford dictionary only shows just over 170,000 English words in current usage. You have a hard time explaining a million smells with 200,000 words—most of which have nothing to do with smell.

Once the wine is in the glass, you want to aerate it by letting some air hit it to release the wonderful flavor compounds. It is a classic image: a group of people lounging around a table, swirling their wine idly, tossing around big and small ideas, and laughing as the conversation wanders around. For some, the swirling helps them think, while for others it is the adult version of a fidget spinner.

But why do we swirl our wine and how do the professionals do it?

Let's step back to a tiny bit of chemistry. The reason wine has those wonderful and complex smells is primarily because of a chemical class known as methoxypyrazines. There are certainly other elements, but these are prevalent and detectable by the human nose at very low levels.

When we swirl, we are opening the wine to air and allowing the smellable elements to volatilize, which lets us smell them. That's the real reason to swirl, to introduce air. It enhances the complexity of the wine by putting all the flavor components the wine has into the air and into our nose.

So, should we swirl? The answer is yes. And there are two main techniques, on the table and the free-hand swirl.

The first is easier and where you should start. The first rule is to make sure your glass isn't too full, perhaps one-third at maximum. This is where those lovely larger glasses come in handy. Even with a decent pour, the wine won't go sloshing over the top.

Place the glass on the table, hold the foot of it, and slowly rotate the glass in small circles. You'll see that the liquid can't quite keep up with your swirling, and you'll get that pretty vortex that sucks in air and lets the aromas flow. This works best when there isn't a tablecloth and the bottom of the glass can move freely. After a few swirls, let it settle and bring the edge of the glass to your nose. Really stick your nose in the glass! Take a nice smell and let it sit. I usually blow that one out to a side and go in for a second one as well because I get even more aromatics on the second sniff than the first as my nose and brain get used to the wine.

PRO TIP

Don't over-swirl.

I mentioned a few swirls, usually three to five, because that is what it takes. The pros don't swirl their wine like they are trying to make a smoothie. One set of swirls, smell and enjoy. Sometimes they'll do it again after the wine has been in the glass a bit to see how it is developing.

The second approach, which is better for experienced swirlers and earlier in the night, is the free-hand swirl. You'll lift the glass, holding the stem, and swirl the bowl, creating the vortex effect. This one is harder because it is way easier to splash over the rim and douse yourself, the table, or your dining companion with your elixir. Trust me, I've done it and been the recipient of a wine bath toward the end of a meal.

Remember, your glass isn't a prop. Fill one-third full, give it three to five good swirls on the table or free hand, and enjoy the wonderful complexity the wine has to offer.

Once the wine is opened, it is ready for the smell. Don't just stick your nose in! This is a delicate process, and you are smelling for compounds that might be available at the parts per million level. Slowly bring the glass to your nose and take a small sniff. Then another. Think of how a dog sniffs to bring scents across his smell receptors. Now, we don't want a bloodhound imitation, but a few gentle sniffs will give you more than one giant inhalation.

Once your nose is over the edge, sniff and then pull back to clear your nose, and go back in for the final good sniff. You'll get different smells on each of the four sniffs, and it will give you a better appreciation for the wine.

Digging deeper, we might be looking for fruit and non-fruit features of the wine to understand where it was made and the choices the winemaker implemented.

Right glass, proper pour, elegant swirl, and little sniffs will have you swirling and sniffing like a pro in no time.

[39]

USING THREE SENSES TO DRINK YOUR WINE

ONE OF THE PARLOR TRICKS that sommeliers use to deepen their appreciation of wine is called deductive tasting. When doing this, they taste a wine "blind," without seeing the label on the bottle. Based on the various sensory input, they will deduce the grape, country, region, quality, and age of the wine. If they are a master sommelier, they will likely be able to name the estate as well.

As impressive as this performance is, it is really designed to deeply understand a wine and deconstruct it so they can accurately and properly describe it to guests. While most wine lovers aren't going to become a sommelier, we can learn from the deductive tasting method used by these experts to appreciate our wine more deeply.

So how do sommeliers evaluate a wine? It's as simple as eyes, nose, mouth. We will follow the deductive tasting technique as we work through the wine.

EYES

The first thing a sommelier will do is evaluate the visual characteristics of a wine: the color, the opacity, the rim variation, and the tears or legs of the wine as it coats the side of the glass. Each of these are indicators of what is to come. For example, a dark, opaque wine is likely to be more powerful than a transparent, light red wine. Edge color can indicate the wine has aged, with red wines becoming lighter as they age and white wines becoming darker.

The legs indicate body and viscosity, with higher viscosity caused by higher alcohol or higher residual sugar.

Eyes	**Factors**
White/Red	Wine color
Gas/Flocculation	Any bubbles?
Clarity/Brightness	Can you see through it?
Rim Color/Staining	Brown or orange edge shows age
Meniscus/Viscosity	How thick is the wine?

NOSE

There are thousands of elements that make up the smell of a wine, and we can use our nose to detect them and learn about a wine. I have talked previously about how to smell your wine, but what are you smelling for? The first thing is flaws to determine if the wine is acceptable. But after that, the fruit components and non-fruit elements are why you smell. Is the fruit first, or is it a secondary component? This can tell you if it is an Old World or New World wine. Is the fruit tart, ripe, or even jammy? Herbs or minerals on the nose? Youthful or clearly aged for a while? All wines have a profile, and over time you will be able to pick up more and more of these elements.

Nose	**Factors**
Clean, correct, no faults?	Is it drinkable?
Fruits	Tree, pit, or tropical fruits? Condition of the fruit
Non-fruits, flowers, herbs, spices, vegetal	Anything besides fruits?

Earth/mineral	Can you smell dirt or rocks?
Wood	Has the wine seen oak?
Intensity/complexity	Goes back to BLIC
Age: young, developed, mature	Your guess on the age

MOUTH

Finally, the taste. Sip a small amount into your mouth and chew the wine to aerate it and release the elements across your palate and into your nose. Do the fruits shift tarter than they were on the nose, or do they get riper? Old World wines tend to get tarter on the tongue from the nose. Are there any other elements in the flavor profile? This is the time to evaluate the acid level of the wine by how quickly it makes you salivate, the body of the wine by how it coats your tongue, and the alcohol level by the burn as you swallow a little. High-alcohol wines taste hotter to us. I learned a great tip from Andy Meyers, a master sommelier, called the "button test." The idea is to take a small swallow of the wine and see how many buttons down on your shirt you feel it burn. The deeper the wine burns, the more alcohol it has in it.

Mouth	**Factor**
Clean, correct, no faults?	Is it drinkable?
Dryness/sweetness	Any sugar in the wine?
Acidity	Does it make you salivate?
Alcohol	How much does it burn?
Body	Lean or round?
Tannin and texture	Does the wine dry out your mouth?
Fruits	Tree, pit, or tropical?

Non-fruits: flower, herbs, spices, vegetal	Anything besides fruits?
Earth/mineral	Can you taste dirt or rocks?
Wood	Has the wine seen oak?
Intensity/complexity	Goes back to BLIC
Balance/length	Goes back to BLIC
Age range	Your guess on the age

Professional sommeliers use their eyes, nose, and mouth to evaluate and analyze the wines they drink. These elements should be in balance and make for a pleasing experience if the winemaker did their job. The next time you pour a glass of something delicious, slow down, and drink the wine with all three senses.

Part Six

GETTING HELP WITH YOUR WINE FROM A PRO

[40]

THE DIFFERENCE BETWEEN A SERVER AND A SOMMELIER

IN EARLIER CHAPTERS I TALKED about asking for a sommelier to help you with the wine list, but why would you do that and under what conditions? Let's start with the people who can help you select a great wine in the restaurant.

The server is always available and sometimes a decent choice. It really depends on their level of training, hopefully under a good sommelier if there is a big wine list. I have found some servers with incredible wine knowledge, but they are generally more senior in the role and have been at that restaurant for a while. Frankly, I am cautious to use a server for advice when I am entertaining important clients, as they will generally go for a safe choice and not something special on the list.

To put this in context, when I waited tables during college, I was often asked to recommend a wine for dinner. Since the place was very beef heavy, I always recommended the same thing, a Mouton Cadet French Bordeaux, a generic, mass-produced red wine from that area. People were usually happy with this pick. My level of wine knowledge at that time? Zero. Another server told me that's what he recommended, so that's what I recommended. I think things are generally a bit better in the modern restaurant scene, but in many cases the knowledge level might only be slightly more than zero.

In a smaller restaurant without a sommelier, the general manager will be curating the wine list, and they will usually have a somewhat broader understanding of the list and what might pair well on the menu. After all, they probably picked the wines. This is a marked upgrade from the server, and it's worth taking the time to have them come over to help. The added benefit of talking to the manager is that your service is likely to be slightly better, as the server knows the manager has met the table.

If available, the sommelier is your best bet, as they will have a deep wine knowledge and specific knowledge of the list. They'll reveal the hidden gems, what is drinking well, and perhaps a wine they are trying to clear out at a bargain price with great P/Q. Ultimately, the sommelier should be running the entire beverage program in the restaurant, picking the wines and spirits, working with the mixologist on special drinks, and training the entire staff on proper service and wine and spirit knowledge. If the waitstaff does a poor job with the beverage service dance, blame the sommelier or the manager, not the server.

It's a great thing when you are fully comfortable ordering wine and cocktails without any help, but if you need some support, my advice is to grab the most knowledgeable person in the restaurant.

[41]

HOW TO TELL YOUR SOMMELIER WHAT KIND OF WINE YOU WANT

THE EASIEST WAY TO TELL a sommelier what type of wine you want is to point to the one that you have selected on the list. Frankly, if you can do that and be comfortable with all the wine styles, you might know more than your server. But that isn't always so easy, and the ability to give some useful guidance can yield you a better wine and dining experience.

There are a few basic approaches to communicating your preference.

Wines You Like: If you have a little wine knowledge and have a few favorites, you are well on your way to clear communication. Let the sommelier know what wines you enjoy, ideally more than one wine you enjoy. This allows them to interpret the style preferences you might like with your meal. The more information you can give, the better odds of ending up with a winner. An example might be, "I enjoy California Zinfandels because of the juicy fruits and the power. I also enjoy Argentinian Malbec for similar reasons."

Regions You Like: A second approach would be to identify the regions that you like because each region has a typical style and the sommelier will use this to make a recommendation. One of the basic breakdowns would be Old World (mostly Europe) and New World (pretty much everywhere else). If you can give additional details, so much the better. An example would be, "We like Northern Rhone wines and have really liked some older Bordeaux as well." That would lead a somm to an Old-World recommendation, though they might suggest an Italian wine to give you a new experience.

PRO TIP

Secretly tell the sommelier your target price by pointing to a price in the list and asking for "something from this region."

Flavors You Like: When sommeliers taste wine, the first thing they look for is fruit, so good guidance might be the fruit profiles that you like in your wines. For white wines, that could be lemon, apple, peach, or tropical fruits. You could also mention if you prefer floral and aromatic wines or more neutral styles. For red wines, it could be red fruits or dark fruits and a comment on some of the funky flavors like mushrooms and leather. If a guest told a sommelier they liked red wines with red fruit and not a lot of funky flavors, they could easily make a recommendation.

Body Styles You Like: The second primary thing sommeliers taste for in wine is the body. This includes acid level, alcohol, tannins, sweetness, body, and texture. Acid is how fast the wine makes you salivate. Alcohol is measured by how far down your throat the wine burns. Tannin is the sensation of drying out your mouth, like strong tea, which has a lot of tannin. Sweetness is the amount of residual sugar left in the wine (which many people confuse with fruitiness). Body is either round or lean, and texture is either lean or creamy. Each of these could be high or low when discussing with the sommelier. A good example is, "I like dry, higher-alcohol wine with good acidity, plenty of tannins, and a lean body."

What You Are Eating: Pairing wine with food is an expertise of a sommelier. If you are flexible about the exact wine you drink, you can just let the sommelier know what everyone is eating, and they will suggest a wine or two for the table.

Surprise Me: If you are an adventurer, you can just put yourself in the hands of the sommelier and ask them to surprise you. Of course, they'll want some guidance on the price, either by asking you or through pointing to a price on the list.

Each of these approaches will help the sommelier get you a wine you'll enjoy!

PRO TIP

Don't ask the sommelier what they like.

While you should trust your sommelier to pick a great wine for you, it can be a big mistake to ask them what they're currently drinking. The reason this can work against you is because these professionals are always looking for something new and different to continue to expand their palate. You have to remember that these folks have sampled thousands of wines, and they might currently be drinking something quite exotic that you won't like at all. I remember a friend who made this mistake and wound up with a glass of orange wine. While this might look like a cool and hip drink, it's not for the faint of heart.

[42]

WHAT DOES A SOMMELIER'S LAPEL PIN MEAN?

YOU CAN TELL A LOT about your sommelier by their lapel pin. Here's a look at the colors of their pins and how it corresponds to what level of certification they have achieved.

RED RIM AND SILVER INTERIOR: INTRODUCTORY

This is the first level at which all prospective master sommeliers begin. It involves a course, followed by a written multiple-choice test. The material covered is extensive, including topics like grapes, winemaking, major wine regions of the world, wine classifications, wine service, and wine pairing with food. This would be an appropriate level for a server in a high-end restaurant.

PURPLE RIM AND PEWTER INTERIOR: CERTIFIED

Now we are getting serious. The certified sommelier qualification is designed for wine and beverage professionals in the hospitality industry wanting a meaningful qualification for the working sommelier. You must have passed the Introductory Class to move on to this level.

The knowledge required is extensive and no one passes without hours of studying. There is a detailed theory test with multiple choice and brief written responses. The candidates must demonstrate wine service that meets the standards of the guild. The most intimidating portion of the test for most people is the blind tasting. They must taste two white and two red wines and must successfully analyze the wines using the standard methodology of the Sommeliers Guild. Ultimately, they should be able to name the grape, country, region, age, and quality of the wines they taste simply through sensory analysis.

Pass all three parts, and you are a Certified Sommelier.

GREEN RIM AND PEWTER INTERIOR: ADVANCED

Now it starts to get hairy. The Advanced Sommelier Certificate course is intended for persons with extensive wine service experience and who wish to develop their knowledge and service skills to a higher level. This is appropriate for someone running the wine program at a very nice restaurant, perhaps even a Michelin-starred restaurant—one of the best in the world.

A few years of dedicated study and immersion in the wine business are needed to pass this test. It involves two and a half days of lecture, followed by two and half days of testing. Once again, wine theory, wine service, and blind tasting of six wines are examined. You must pass all three sections, or you start this level all over again. The master sommeliers who offer the test are also looking at demeanor and skill with diners, asking difficult questions. An advanced sommelier should be able to handle almost anything related to wine.

RED RIM AND GOLD INTERIOR: MASTER

To illustrate how hard it is to get a Master Sommelier designation, I want to put this in perspective: There have been 533 people who have traveled into outer space since 1960. There have only been 236 people who have achieved Master Sommelier status worldwide since 1969. It's that hard!

The format of the test is the same as for the Advanced Certification, but the level of knowledge, tasting, and service are pushed to a whole new level. Odd wines from smaller countries could be on the test, unruly guests with difficult demands might appear in the service section, and the theory testing is anything but straightforward. The good news is that you can pass the test in parts, so if you pass a section, you don't have to go back and take it again.

Next time you are at a nice restaurant, check the lapel pin on your wine steward. You'll have a new appreciation for the work and knowledge they put in to earn that designation. And if you have a highly certified sommelier, put yourself in their hands. They will make sure you have a great wine experience.

[43]

GOOD SOMMELIER VS. BAD SOMMELIER

A GOOD SOMMELIER CAN BE your best ally when it comes to choosing your wine. That said, not every sommelier has your best interests in mind. Here are a couple of examples of how a good sommelier contrasts with a bad one.

- A good sommelier helps you find a wine at the price point you want to spend. A bad sommelier pushes you to spend more than you want to.
- A good sommelier will explain if the vintage of a wine is a good one—or not. A bad sommelier will just try to move their inventory.
- A good sommelier fills everyone's glass just enough—about a third of the glass. A bad sommelier will pour more, quickly emptying the bottle, to push you to order another bottle or because they are being lazy and want to reduce their trips to the table.
- A good sommelier always makes time for your questions. A bad sommelier makes you feel like your questions are imposing on them.
- A good sommelier checks back on your table often to make sure you're enjoying your wine. You won't see a bad sommelier again after your initial order.
- A good sommelier will never fight you if you think a bottle is corked. In fact, they'll apologize and take it right away. A bad sommelier will fight you until the end.

- If you bring a bottle of wine to the restaurant, a good sommelier will be happy to help you open it. A bad sommelier will give you the stink-eye and make you feel like you're stealing from them.

[44]

HOW DO YOU TIP ON WINE?

AT SOME BUSINESS DINNERS, WINE can make up more than 50 percent of the total bill and that leaves the host to wonder, "How should I tip on the wine?" Should I tip less on the wine and blend the overall tip, or should I tip the sommelier separately? This is especially true if the sommelier did a particularly good job.

Let's back up and investigate how sommeliers are paid. There are differences between a floor sommelier or manager and someone running the entire wine program. Certification level makes a difference as well. A typical certified floor somm will make an average of $60,000 a year, based on the 2015 Guildsomm Salary Survey. This is comprised of daily base pay and tips. Meanwhile, a Master Sommelier who is running the wine program can make up to $147,000 a year. The base pay can range from $275 a day for a certified somm to $1,000 a day for a master somm (it pays to study!).

The difference between the daily base salary and the total compensation is made up from tips. There are two strategies that restaurants use to pay their sommeliers. The first is to compensate them on the wine and alcohol sold. This makes sense as that is their primary job, and due to the profitability of wine and spirits, the owner wants someone solely focused on driving sales of these profitable items. This can range from 5 to 10 percent of the sales, depending on the establishment, the certification level, and the experience of the sommelier. The commission is paid by the house. In high-end restaurants with a great wine list, this can be very lucrative.

PRO TIP

Sommeliers are paid on liquor sales.

The second approach is to have the sommelier in the tip pool with the wait staff. This makes some sense as in most restaurants, the somm is either the manager or a high-level floater to help the service. This means they are clearing plates, bussing tables, and bringing new silverware—basically whatever is needed to give a great experience. In this model, the sommelier is tipped out at the end of the night, and the rate can range from 1 to 3 percent of the total tip pool. For more moderate places, this is a better deal for the sommelier as the food is a bigger part of the average bill.

Finally, some places blend the two approaches and provide a portion of the tip pool and a payment from the house based on wine and spirit sales. This will typically run 2 percent of the pool and perhaps another 3 to 5 percent of the wine sales.

PRO TIP

Sommeliers are paid from table tips or all spirit sales, so you don't have to tip them separately

This leaves us with the question of how to tip these specialized servers. Typical etiquette is to tip on the total amount as you normally might, such as 15 to 20 percent for good service. No adjustment is made for the value of the wine. One way to think about this is if you brought your own bottle into the restaurant, you'd pay a corkage fee of $25 to $50, which is around the tip level for a nice bottle. Based on either of the approaches above, the sommelier should be taken care of by either the tip pool or a payment from the house for the wine sold.

Sometimes, when you get a little crazy with the wine, ordering ancient Bordeaux or magnums of cult California Cabs, you can reduce the overall tip amount to the 10 to 15 percent range. The sommelier will appreciate the chance to taste some of your wine if it is special and spectacular, and that will suffice as an incremental tip.

PRO TIP

For great service, a $20 to $50 tip can make sense for the sommelier.

If the somm did a very nice job, you can find them after the meal and give them a cash tip on top of the tip for the bill. A tip of $20 to $50 is well appreciated and more than the money is recognition for a nice job. Believe me, the next time you come to that place, the sommelier will remember you and make a great effort to ensure you have a wonderful time.

[45]

TOP 19 THINGS YOUR SOMMELIER WISHED YOU KNEW

I ASKED DOZENS OF WINE professionals and sommeliers what they wished their clients knew. That list of distilled wisdom is captured in this Top 19 list.

1. My goal is to find the best bottle of wine for your budget, not the most expensive bottle on the list—unless that's what you want. A good sommelier will pair the wine to the customer's tastes, preferences, and pocketbook. After all, the sommelier wants a happy customer who will recommend him to others, not complain about him or their experience.
2. When I pour them a taste of the wine, the purpose is not to pass it around the table and decide if everyone likes it.
3. Don't be embarrassed. You don't have to be an expert to have an opinion and being shy about your preferences won't help either of us. Don't worry about using the right vocabulary. Our job is to make you look good in front of your guests.
4. If you find a restaurant with a good half-bottle program, take advantage of it. It gives you way more flexibility with pairings, and you get to try more things.
5. Don't be afraid of the blends. A lot of people are going for single varietal wines because they think they know the grape and what to expect. Don't be afraid to try weird, unknown, indigenous wines from around the world. It's not just France and Italy. It might be more possible to get

satisfaction from a Lebanese Cinsault than a random Bordeaux Supérieur.

6. I have some customers who ask for wines that are "not acidic," because they don't understand that acidity is an essential component in a balanced wine. And that if the acidity feels too strong, it is probably because most wine is meant to be paired with food.
7. They should know at least what sort of wine they like and what is their taste. That would be helpful for a sommelier to recommend wines similar or something close to wines they have tried before.
8. Stop worrying about point scores. They are only useful if you have the exact same taste in wine as Robert Parker.
9. If you don't like Chardonnay, try it again. It's delicious and deserves your love. Also, not every Chardonnay is oaked or packed with dairy flavor.
10. Riesling is amazing, especially with food, and it isn't always sweet. (I just saw a T-shirt that said, "If You Don't Like Riesling, You're F**king Stupid.")
11. If you and your friends like wine, start a tasting group. It's the best way to learn.
12. Only the sommelier really knows their own list: what are the deals, what is showing well, the up-the-sleeve selections. They can match something you have had or help you explore a new wine. They know the menu and the chef's style for pairing with the flavors.
13. Talk to the sommelier. Please. It's our job, and we do it because we love it. The restaurants pay us to provide this service, so take advantage.
14. A price indication is important. I love it when a guest points to a bottle on the list and says, "We would like something like this, but we are having X. Would this be a good pairing? Or what would you recommend?"

15. Do not ask, "What is the best wine on the menu?" Should I say the incredibly expensive bottle of Petrus? Better details to guide a sommelier include what you are having, your budget, and the style of wine that you like. The correct context dictates what is best.
16. Try to be open-minded about wine. Go out of your comfort zone. You will be surprised and delighted! Open-minded guests end up with better wine.
17. Don't be intimidated, either by the wine list or the sommelier. Both are there to ensure that you find a wine that complements your meal.
18. We got into this profession because we love the product. That's it. We could make a lot more money doing a great many more things.
19. Yes, we have seen the movie *Somm*...

Part Seven

EXPAND YOUR COLLECTION AND YOUR PALATE

[46]

14 WINES FOR A PROFESSIONAL DRINKING CELLAR

IN CHAPTER THIRTEEN, WE COVERED the Seven Noble Grapes. These are the international varietals that are grown all over the world and represent the basics of wine. If you want to start a good cellar with excellent diversity, you can use these grapes as your starting point. The other element you will want to consider is Old World and New World styles of wine. (For more, see Chapter Fifteen.)

You can build a wonderful and comprehensive cellar to expand your palate or to entertain clients and friends at home from these two ideas. With 14 wines, seven Old World and seven New World, you'll have a collection that can please almost anyone. Of course, you can branch out from here and add all your favorites. I'd immediately add Chianti and some Champagne, for example.

Keep notes as you try all these wines. After you have tasted your way through these, you'll have a great understanding of what you like and what you don't. You can use your notes at your next business dinner to tell the sommelier what you like, or at the local wine store to get guidance on other wines you might like. More importantly, you'll be able to please the palate of almost any guest who arrives at your home.

Old World Wines

Grape	Classic Example
Chardonnay	French Chablis
Sauvignon Blanc	French Sancerre
Riesling	German Mosel
Cabernet Sauvignon	French Medoc Bordeaux
Pinot Noir	French Burgundy
Merlot	French Saint Emillion Bordeaux
Syrah	French Cote Rotie

New World Wines

Grape	Best Region
Chardonnay	Sonoma Chardonnay
Sauvignon Blanc	New Zealand Sauvignon Blanc
Riesling	Australian Riesling
Cabernet Sauvignon	Napa Cabernet Sauvignon
Pinot Noir	Oregon Pinot Noir
Merlot	Napa Merlot
Syrah	Australian Shiraz

It's a fair critique that I left out a few hundred amazing wine areas and a few thousand great grapes. Guilty as charged. But that expansive thinking about wine is exactly what paralyzes us at the wine store. Humans can't process so many choices, and a narrow focus can get you some great outcomes.

Once you are comfortable with what you like, get crazy and try the same grapes from other areas or different grapes from the same area. A moderately priced bottle isn't that big a financial commitment. Remember, wine is supposed to be fun.

[47]

WHAT MAKES A WINE AGE-WORTHY?

IT'S A BASIC QUESTION: "CAN I leave this wine in my cellar for a while or do I need to drink it now?" I get it all the time when I talk to friends with a few wines in storage, and they are worried about their nice wine turning into not-so-nice vinegar. There are a few things that an age-worthy wine needs.

When wine experts are tasting wines, they categorize the flavors into three chunks. Primary flavors are things that came from the vineyard; they were in the fruit, the ground, and the place. These are the lovely fruity notes in wine. Secondary flavors were developed in the winery, by the choices of the winemaker. One example might be if the wine was stored in oak, the type of oak, and how long it was stored. The winemaker makes dozens of decisions to optimize what they put in the bottle. Tertiary flavors are things that develop over time in the bottle—in other words, from aging. Caramel and nutty notes in a white wine and tobacco and coffee in a red wine are examples of tertiary flavors. These flavors are less predictable and part of what makes a wine so variable.

These unique tertiary notes are what we are seeking when we age a wine. They weren't in the original wine that we got from the winery; they developed over time with slow chemical reactions that happen in the bottle. For our purposes, there must be at least two things present for these fun reactions to occur.

The first thing that must be present is oxygen. Low, steady availability of oxygen is one of the critical ingredients to aging wine. It turns out there is an almost perfect device available to let a low, steady amount of oxygen into a wine bottle. A cork! It is microporous and nature lets just the right amount through to slowly age a wine. The corollary to this is:

PRO TIP

A wine with a screwcap doesn't age.

Since no air is allowed through the nearly perfect seal created by a screwcap, the wine is almost exactly as it left the winery. That makes them perfect for bright red and white wines that want to present vibrant fruit and the energy in the grapes.

The wine also needs either high acid or high tannins to have the structure to age over time. A low-acid wine or a wine without tannins is unlikely to age well. Generally, this means a white wine with mouthwatering acids when it is bottled or a red white with mouth-puckering tannins are the raw material for an age-worthy wine. This means the wine might not be in balance when you first taste it, but the winemaker is designing a wine to develop over time and be at its peak years after bottling.

In Chapter Forty-nine, I cover proper storage of your wine, but it really hits home here. These wonderful flavor-developing reactions progress best at cellar temperature, and more importantly the yummy molecules that develop are very delicate and can easily be destroyed by heat. If you want to age your wine, keep it in proper storage conditions.

Frankly, I am impatient to drink my great wine. Life is short and it's Tuesday, so why not open that great bottle with your burgers?

[48]

NEVER BUY FRESH WINE AGAIN

THERE'S A FAMOUS LINE FROM the movie *The Jerk* where Steve Martin finishes a bottle of 1966 Château Latour Bordeaux, and the waiter asks if he would like another. Martin says no, he'd like to splurge and get some fresh stuff, "No older than this year."

While we laugh at how ignorant Steve Martin's character is, a lot of wine collectors end up doing something similar. They go to their favorite retailer, walk the shelves, and purchase a vintage from what they have available. Unfortunately, due to the need to turn inventory, most of those bottles are just a few years old—straight from the winemaker. If a store is investing in age-worthy wines, the hapless wine buyer will be laying those precious bottles down in their cellars, so they can drink them in 10 or even 15 years!

PRO TIP

Most retail shops only have fresh wine.

Another example of a wine collector behaving badly is the Bordeaux futures lottery. In April of each year, the wines from the prior year are tasted while still in the barrel by critics who are hoping to determine if the wine will be great or not. This system allows the buyer to purchase the right to buy that wine, which will be delivered in two years.

The wine estates use this to finance their operations in a way that is cheaper than going to the bank. They have their wine already sold as it slowly ages in the barrel or bottle. Great for them, and not bad for the buyer if the year is good. The problem is, not every year is great, and the critics' barrel tasting isn't a guarantee that the year is amazing. That said, lots of people love this participation in the wine process and hope that they win the lottery by getting an amazing year for less than they would pay when the bottles hit the market.

This lottery allows the buyer the privilege of storing the wine for 10, 15, or even 20 years before it is ready to drink. That's risking a lot of money for a wine that might be just above average. A steely-eyed businessperson would question this in terms of net present value of the decision.

Luckily, there is a better way.

What many sophisticated buyers are doing is going to auction houses and buying aged, ready-to-drink wine from known good years. This eliminates the risk that the year is poor. It also allows someone else to age the wine for you in their cellar until it is ready to drink and finance that aging.

An example of this would be the 2014 Château Cos d'Estournel. This is a second growth from Bordeaux and a personal favorite of mine. Early reviews indicated the 2014 would be an excellent vintage, with scores in the high 90s. It was originally available on a futures contract for $119 a bottle. While it was delivered in late 2017, it won't be ready to drink until perhaps 2030, when, after 13 years of aging, it will be on the early edge of drinkability. Your kindergarten-aged child will be graduating high school when you crack the first bottle!

If you went to an auction house, you could buy a 1996 Château Cos d'Estournel for $159 a bottle, plus a little shipping. This was a great year and with over 20 years of age, it is ready to drink now!

Now for the finance geeks, let's calculate the net present value of that 2014 bottle we can buy for $119 but need to age 20 years before we can drink it. When you do the math, 20 years with a nominal 5 percent interest rate puts the cost of drinking that bottle at $315. When you consider that you can buy a ready-to-drink bottle of the 1996 vintage for about half that price, you see what an incredible bargain it is.

PRO TIP

Aged wine comes from private cellars.

Where does this great aged wine come from? Dead guys, usually. And sometimes older collectors who have figured out that they can never drink all the wine they have, and they are rotating out a portion of their older wines that really need to be drunk soon. Their loss is your gain as these older wines, with age and ready to drink, come at a very reasonable price compared to purchasing new. The best part is that you can check the reviews on the year of the wine to confirm that they have been vetted as exceptional, avoiding any chance of buying wine from a bad year.

Don't be like *The Jerk* and buy the fresh stuff. Go to the auction houses and buy known great vintages that you can drink shortly after they arrive in the mail.

[49]

STORING YOUR WINE

WHEN IT COMES TO STORING wine you've bought and brought home to drink later, the optimum conditions are 50-degree Fahrenheit and 50 percent humidity. Why? Because corks are semi-permeable; some oxygen gets into the wine over time. Not too much, but just enough. This can be a good thing as it triggers an aging of the wine where new flavors develop that weren't there originally.

You need to think back to your high school chemistry class to understand the reasons that the temperature and humidity levels are relevant. Any time you increase the temperature by 20 degrees Fahrenheit, you double the reaction speed. That means if you put your wine on top of your fridge where it's 90 degrees, your wine will age four times as fast as it will if you store it at 50 degrees. That rapid aging typically results in weird funky flavors developing—or wine that quickly turns into vinegar.

A lot of people rely on wine fridges these days to control temperature. But these devices don't do much when it comes to humidity control or limiting how much light your wine is exposed to. That's why a great place to store your wine is in your basement—preferably near a dirt wall and far from your furnace.

KEEPING TRACK OF YOUR WINE AT HOME

One of the easiest ways to keep track of the wine you've bought and when you bought it is by using a spreadsheet. You can just log the vintage along with the price you paid and the date you made the purchase. But there are now multiple apps available to help you keep on top of your wine inventory as well. One of them is called Vivino, which lets you take a picture of the label. The app then matches the label with its database to collect all the relevant information, including any comments or ratings you want to add. This can be a great way to track what you drink as well as what you might want to buy again later.

Another app, which integrates with Vivino, is called Cellar Tracker. Like Vivino, Cellar Tracker uses your phone's camera to take pictures of wine bottle labels. The app then calculates the optimum drinking window for your wine, which can be very helpful in managing what you drink and when to drink it.

[50]

GREAT PLACES TO BUY OLDER WINES

I love to drink aged wines, but I am also impatient and don't want to wait 10 or even 15 years for them to get into their prime. This clearly causes me a problem. Luckily, there are several online retailers that specialize in these older gems that have a great selection of ready-to-drink age-worthy wines for you to grab today and enjoy at your next special dinner.

Now, they don't buy young wines and lay them down for many years, waiting for the peak of drinkability either. Usually, these vendors specialize in buying larger cellars from big collectors of wine. Sometimes this happens when a collector shifts their tastes over time, or sometimes it happens after they pass on and their estate is liquidating a very large liquid asset. In either case, you are the beneficiary of these amazing collections, lovingly gathered and hopefully carefully aged.

The good news is that part of the value provided by the retailer is a careful inspection of the bottles to ensure they are not fake and that they are in reasonable condition. They can't certify the wine isn't corked; that is the buyer's risk—but that's always the case. They usually know the collector and sometimes check the storage conditions to make sure that the wines have been properly cared for during their aging process. If there has been deterioration of the wine level or the label, they will usually note that in the description.

There are two basic business models that are used in this space: retail and auction. In the retail model, they buy the wines and mark them up to appropriate levels for the age and condition of the wines. There is a secondary market for most wines, so they can't get too crazy as you can check more than one site to ensure the price is fair. If you want the bottle, you pay the price and it is yours.

In the auction model, the bottles are usually consigned to the seller and they promote the wines in regular sales, attracting lots of buyers. Christie's and Hart Davis Hart are two of the larger firms that do auction style. The buyers bid up the price to whatever level they choose until the sale closes. Usually, there are online bids with maximum prices they are willing to offer. These are then matched against the people at the live auction on the day of the sale. Whichever stays longest and highest wins the wine. The auction house will then add a buyer's premium of 20 to 25 percent, which is the margin for the auction house for all their work, so factor this in when you bid.

Some of these houses specialize in full cases with the original wooden cases. While these are great looking in your cellar, they do come at a slight premium. If you are only about the wine, you will spend a bit less for partial cases.

Christie's—New York & London: Christie's is a broad-based auction house that sells everything from Warhols to wine. They have specialists who curate the wine they sell and verify the pedigree. They specialize in European wines and ancient vintages. *christies.com*

Hart Davis Hart—Chicago: This is the place to go for epic wine in old wooden cases. If you want first-growth Bordeaux, premium Burgundy, or legendary Napa Cabernets, try here. It attracts interest from around the world, so there aren't many bargains, but the selection is great. It's almost worth registering to get the catalog, as it has incredible wine photos. *hdhwine.com*

The Chicago Wine Company—Wooddale, Illinois: The Chicago Wine Company is a blended business, offering retail and auction sales. They have more partial cases of wine, which tend to go a little cheaper than 12-bottle cases in original wooden cases. They also have a regular email if you have a style of wine you like to drink, alerting you to new acquisitions. *tcwc.com*

Benchmark Wine—Napa, California: Benchmark buys cellars from collectors of fine wines. As a buyer, you have them representing the bona fides for the wine, including condition and storage of the bottles. They have a great interface and a newsletter that will alert a buyer of types of wines. This is one of my favorites. *benchmarkwine.com*

K&L Wine Merchants—Redwood, California: This California retailer has been serving collectors for more than 30 years. It's like having an amazing wine store in your neighborhood with a great web interface and real-time inventory data, so you know they have the bottles you want. They drink all the wine they represent and give comments and knowledgeable insight. Deeper in Californian wines, they have a good selection of Europeans and direct purchases as well. *klwines.com*

Flickinger Wines—Chicago: Flickinger retails fine and rare vintages of great world wines with excellent selection, provenance, price, and service. They have an extensive inventory of Bordeaux, Burgundy, Rhone, Italy, California, Lebanon, Spain, Vintage Port, and Australia. They have very competitive pricing. They have solid interface and a regular newsletter for alerts. *flickingerwines.com*

Domaine Storage—Saint Louis: Domaine started as a storage firm for private collections and has morphed into a seller of private collections as a service and now a business. They sell retail and have a wide selection of collectibles. They also offer other services around wine, including storage, insurance, selling, buying, and shipping. *domainestorage.com*

If you want to build your cellar and drink some amazing wine, give one of these places a try. They have big collections of aged and ready-to-drink wines.

[51]

ACCESSING LIBRARY WINES FROM GREAT ESTATES

IT'S A LITTLE SECRET OF the winemaking business: makers don't sell all the wine from their production. They'll typically hold back 10 to 20 percent for future release. These bottles sit sleeping quietly in the makers' personal caves and storage areas for 20, 30, 50, or even more years! I've seen video of European winemakers pulling out some wines that were 100 years old and drinking great. The question is, besides buying the winery, how do we access these incredible gems?

There are a few techniques that you'll want to know to find a truly special wine. If you're looking for a birth-year wine or an anniversary wine, you might need to use all these approaches, and add a healthy dose of patience. Oh, and don't forget a few sacks of gold because this won't be cheap.

BUY AT AUCTION

The prior chapter is about auction houses, and it's a great way to access older vintages. The beauty here is that they have generally been collected and properly stored by a knowledgeable collector. Now, that's no guarantee that the wine is correct. Even perfect storage sometimes yields a bad bottle, but the better houses will stand behind the provenance of their product.

PRO TIP

Aged wine comes from the cellars of winemakers.

BE ON THE LIST

Wineries love the people who love them. So how do you give love to a winery? Simple: Buy lots of their wine. All the premium wineries have mailing lists, and people who have been on the list for many years—particularly ones who are volume purchasers—get their attention.

I have a friend who is a huge purchaser of Del Dotto Wines. I suspect that Dwayne is the top buyer for this winery, even ahead of most restaurants almost every year. When he calls and asks for a special wine, perhaps a few bottles of 30-year-old wine to celebrate an anniversary, believe me—they try to deliver!

JUST ASK

I was recently speaking with a few makers of epic Napa wines, and they had another suggestion for accessing library wines: "Just ask!" We are all human, and if you have a great reason and a story, sometimes a bottle of that 50-year-old Napa Cabernet can be found somewhere in the cellar. If you were celebrating 25 years being cancer free, for example, and wanted a single bottle of your favorite wine to celebrate, I know I'd try my best to find one if I had a cellar full!

If you are a longtime client and supporter, your odds are way better, but it never hurts to ask. The worst they can say is, "No."

KNOW A SOMMELIER

As a corollary to the second idea of being a big client, having a big client ask for you can work as well. If you have a favorite restaurant, and I mean one that you know the general manager and sommelier by first name, you have an opening. I'd study their list and see what wineries their big suppliers are. Then go to the sommelier and ask if they can get a bottle of that special vintage from a large supplier. If they are deep in that wine and ask for you, there is a good shot they will be able to produce.

If your favorite sommelier did you a solid and got you that wine you wanted, you should consider having the event at that restaurant. At a minimum, you should come up with a great tip next time you dine there, and I'd definitely suggest offering a taste of that well-aged wine to the sommelier as a thank you for getting it.

Getting an aged wine isn't an everyday occurrence, but if you want to really celebrate, it's a great way to make the event special.

[52]

EXPAND YOUR PALATE WITH A WINE CLUB

CAN YOU REMEMBER THE FIRST wine that you fell in love with and the first time you sipped it? The ephemeral experience of a wine that tickled all the right spots, made you want another sip, and caused you to become a fan? When that happens, it often becomes one of your go-to wines. When we hit the store trying to find a wine for an event or to share with friends, we browse the aisles and end up... exactly at the same spot, with our old friend, our go-to wine.

Why?

Because a typical wine store might have 500 different bottles while a superstore might have thousands! How can you decide? You've never tasted most of them and don't want to invest your money in something you don't like. Or worse, you don't want to bring something to a friend's home only to find that it is horrible (although we must remember, there is no bad wine!).

There's a better and less risky way to expand your palate and have some fun doing it: Join a wine club. There are a bunch in the market, but some of the best ones have taken notes from Uber and Netflix to develop great software and algorithms to find the perfect wine for you.

You usually sign up for a monthly subscription of two to four bottles, depending on your consumption. Depending on the club, this will cost you $30 to $100 a month. The price will depend on how much the underlying wines cost, which isn't always correlated to quality.

The newer wine clubs will have you answer several questions about your taste profile to help them select great wines you will enjoy. These questions aren't about wine, but rather focused on things like if you like sugar in your coffee or if you like spicy food. All these questions are designed to give them hints as to your palate. Basically, they are going to curate your wine selection and help you along the path.

Like Netflix, once the wines arrive and you try them, you are supposed to rate the wines based on how you liked them. Over time, they learn your preferences and can home in on some great wines you will enjoy. And while you do, you'll try some things you would never have pulled off the shelves at the local liquor store. After a few months, when you're ready to try something new, you can head into your local wine store with a new confidence as you look for the grapes and growing areas that you enjoyed thanks to your experience with the club. But this time, you'll have the confidence of having tried something similar and knowing you like the taste.

Winc (Previously Club W) from Playa Vista, California, is one of these new-style wine clubs. They developed the business by looking hard at the target customers and figuring out what they were missing in the wine experience. They attempt to deliver exploration, context, and cultural relevance with all their wines. That means they offer wines from around the world, such as good benchmark wines from Albarinos to Pinot Noir to sparkling Rosé. They explain what the wines are and where they came from to give them context and include great recipes to pair with your newfound wine.

They also have a sophisticated taste-matching system and a wide variety of more than 20 wines they curate. What is unique about Winc is that they have vertically integrated back to the grapes, winemaking, and bottling, unlike most wine clubs. This means they can deliver great price-to-quality ratios and give you a tour of wines around the world with reliable quality levels. The only downside is if you like a wine, you can't go down to your local store and grab some more. But Winc is working to fix that by developing retail distribution of their most popular wines. They average around $13 a bottle for their selections. *Winc.com*

Cellars Wine Club is a premium wine club for those who have a better feel for what they like. You can select from single-bottle shipments up to cases on the shipment schedule you select. They have some fun categories, including the 90+ Point Wine selection, the Sparkling Wine Club, and the higher-end Connoisseur Club. Wines range up to $40 a bottle for the more selective clubs. You can check them out at *cellarswineclub.com*

The appropriately named **Bright Cellars** was created by two MIT grads with a passion for wine. They have a Bright Points algorithm that scores each wine by comparing 18 attributes to your preferences, matching you with your monthly experience. They bring in wines from producers around the world and package them into a four-bottle-per-month shipment for around $15 a bottle. Find them at *brightcellars.com*

Tasting Room has a unique approach to determining your palate by sending you a package of six smaller, airline-sized bottles of wine. You are supposed to taste them, rate them, and report back to Tasting Room. They will use this data to develop your first shipment. You can select the quantity of wines you want in each shipment and the frequency of shipment. They will select from their 62 producer-direct wines to tickle your taste buds. You might have seen them on TV. You can start now at *tastingroom.com*

Wall Street Journal Wine Club is one of the original wine clubs and follows the traditional model of curating great wines from a variety of producers around the world. You can pick whites, reds, or mixed cases of wine. They offer classic grape varieties from each area, so you become grounded in the differences between French and Californian Cabernet Sauvignon. It hits the sweet spot for quarterly wine clubs, with an average price of around $14 a bottle, delivered. They have a cheaper price to get you started. *wsjwine.com*

Whichever wine club you select, it's a great way to open your palate to new choices and gain confidence as you head to the wine store. Pick one and give it a go!

[53]

WINE TASTING WITH FRIENDS

If you're not ready to invest in a wine club, consider expanding your palate by tasting wine with friends. This is one of the ways sommeliers grow their wine knowledge. They taste a broad diversity of wines, lots of grapes from lots of regions. You can easily emulate this yourself.

A TASTING GROUP

Have some friends who want to expand their wine knowledge? Invite them over. The usual rule is that everyone brings a bottle to share with the group, and they must know something about what they brought so they can share the wine and the knowledge. This doesn't have to break the bank. There are lots of wines with great typicity under $20 a bottle.

As the host, you set the theme for the wines. Perhaps California Chardonnays, or Old-World Wines, or Rhone wines, or even sweet wines. It's really your call, and hopefully over time you cover a gamut of wines you might have never tried. Some you'll love and others you won't enjoy as much (remember, there is no bad wine). A more structured approach would be to use the wines on the Certified Sommelier Test, which has an excellent diversity of typical wines. You can find links to the testable reds and whites at professionaldrinking.com

Once you have selected the theme for the wines, the host provides the glassware, some nibbles, and a spit bucket. (Yes, you should spit.) I like to have plenty of water around to keep hydrated and cleanse palates.

Usually one person reviews the wine: visually, smell, and taste. Once they have weighed in, others can chime in with their views and if they had the same experience. You can do this open, where you know the wine, or blind, where it is revealed after the tasting is done. I like to wrap my bottles in aluminum foil to hide their identity, because I always have aluminum foil in my kitchen unlike a brown paper bag, and it stays put until I want to show off my bottle.

PRO TIP

If you are tasting wine, you are spitting—otherwise you are drinking.

If you really want to taste like a sommelier, you can use the Deductive Tasting Method to focus on each element of the wine—eyes, nose, and taste. You'll find a link to this at professionaldrinking.com as well. The further benefit of the grid is that is gives you language to describe what you are smelling and tasting. That's usually the thing most people need help on.

PRO TIP

Buy on apples; sell on cheese.

When you're tasting wine, it's best to have a clean palate so you can really taste the wine. One way to clean your palate is by eating apples. You can also drink a little Champagne to freshen things up. What you want to avoid, however, is eating cheese. All wine tastes good with cheese! That's why a winery will put it out for you to sample. But this can be a trap because you'll think the wine is great, but later after you've brought the bottle home, you experience some buyer's regret. It's okay to eat the cheese—after you've already made your buying decisions, or after you have finished tasting and have moved on to just drinking.

VISITING A WINERY

I feel the need to offer some special advice when you visit a winery as part of a professional drinking event—especially if it involves visiting multiple wineries in places like Napa Valley. One obvious tip here is avoid driving: hire a bus or an Uber to ensure you're not driving while drinking.

The other tip is that you're there to taste the wine—not to drink it. Consider that a typical tasting involves trying four to six different wines. If you repeat that three or four times, you might be in serious trouble. That's why I encourage you to take advantage of the spittoon. It's there for a reason. Sommeliers are spitting out wine all the time. The point is not to drink all the wine they put in front of you. To help avoid temptation, I will even take a sip and then pour the rest of the glass into the spittoon. Your goal should be to find wines you think are delicious and then either buy a few bottles to bring home with you or ask to have them shipped to your house.

Part Eight
ENTERTAINING AT HOME

[54]

THE DECISION TO ENTERTAIN AT HOME OR A RESTAURANT

IF YOU ARE A CONFIRMED restaurant entertainer and never plan to bring anyone to your home, you can skip this chapter. For many of us, when we are developing a relationship or we like the people we are doing business with, we might want to invite them to our home.

Nothing sets the tone for a quality conversation more than the place. When picking the venue for your next meeting over a meal, you need to think carefully as it communicates something about the nature of the meeting as well as your judgment. Should you pick your local bar, where everyone knows your name and the buffalo wings are to die for? Or should you hit the 14-course tasting menu at Chez Fifi, which will set you back several sacks of gold? It depends.

The first thing to consider is the nature of the meeting you are about to have. That means the objective, the need for important conversations, and how much you have developed the relationship. Here are a few of the most typical scenarios to give you a guide.

Introductory: This is a time for conversation, sharing about families, hobbies, the basics of your businesses, and potentially areas to work together. This is better done at a restaurant.

Interview: An interview is close to the introductory meeting for the location, except many times it will be lunch. This type of meeting should never happen at home. A more neutral location is better.

Relationship Building: Once a relationship has been established and that delicate dance is over, you can get more creative and the options open for a business meeting.

One great option if you enjoy entertaining, and your significant other is game, is to invite people to your home. It is a chance to show off some culinary skills and open your wine cellar or show off your signature cocktail. This level of intimacy can drive a business relationship to whole new levels. Do not do this casually, as it should be reserved for people you genuinely enjoy and with whom you want a long-term friendship. I'll usually wait until the third meeting or even later before inviting anyone to my home.

Deal Making: I avoid deal making in my home as it is an unbalanced venue. I am in my home, comfortable, and I know where everything is. My guest must ask where the bathroom is located. It isn't the place to have a partnership conversation.

Celebrating: Celebrating can be done at your home, whether the group is small or large. My advice for smaller groups is to have everything prepared in advance, so you can focus on your guests rather than the food. For a larger celebration, it's time to call the caterer, even if that means a platter of Chick-fil-A chicken sandwiches.

[55]

A BASIC BAR AND WINE CELLAR SET-UP

IF YOU HAVE MADE THE decision to entertain in your home, you'll need a basic bar for your company in case they'd like a drink. Wine is likely to be on tap for the meal, but if you are thinking cocktails, you'll need the following:

Glasses: A set of nice glasses. Don't worry about perfect glasses for every drink, but they should be glass, without a logo of your favorite baseball team. Make sure to have a few smaller ones for straight liquor and a few larger ones for mixed drinks.

Liquor: You don't need to have every alcohol under the sun, but a bottle of vodka, gin, whiskey (any kind), single malt scotch, and bourbon would be the minimum. You can make a bunch of drinks with these five bottles. I try to develop a fun cocktail that I'll serve to everyone who wants one. That could be a gin and tonic or a martini, but it makes things easier if you are limiting the options.

Mixers: Many of the above liquors can be drunk straight up or with some water, but you'll probably want a few mixers to set up the basic cocktails. Tonic water, club soda, ginger ale, and vermouth are in my bar always. Sometimes I'll add another mixer or two if I am making a special cocktail.

Beer: I mentioned before that beer is a great starter, particularly on a summer evening. If you're entertaining, get a six-pack each of two fancier beers of different styles.

[56]

HOW MUCH WINE TO HAVE ON HAND

WHEN YOU ARE PREPARING TO entertain and get all your adult beverages organized, how much wine to have on hand might cross your mind.

If you have a deep wine cellar, or you have invested in my 14-bottle wine cellar from Chapter Forty-six, you have plenty of wine except for blowout parties.

When calculating the correct amount of wine, you need to take a few things into account, including the number of people coming, the length of the party, and if you know the crowd, how heavily they drink.

PRO TIP

Plan for half a bottle of wine per person.

That adds up to three four-ounce pours per person, which are modest by current standards. This rule would work for moderate drinkers over a two-hour event. An example would be a standing event with passed trays of food.

When I am having people over for an evening, I'll bump this up to a bottle per person. I know that is likely too much, as there are always non-drinkers in the crowd and many people stop after two drinks. I don't mind since the extra goes into my cellar for later consumption. My rule of thumb is to over-order, so I don't run out and buzzkill the event.

PRO TIP

Buy wine you'll be happy to drink later.

Since I know I'll have leftover wine, I am careful to get wine that I'll be happy to have later, either over a meal or with friends at a future get-together. That means I'll get a better caliber of wine for most gatherings. My guests benefit from this better wine, and no one has every complained about my selections—a great win-win solution!

If the group is made up of heavy drinkers, and if the party is designed to go all night, I'll plan for a bottle per person and have a few in reserve. I once hosted a tasting for a television personality, and their group blew through all the wine I brought, plus two spares. We were many bottles into their wine cellar before I claimed it was a school night and had to leave. I don't ever want to run out of wine unless I want everyone to go home when I am tired—then I am happy to "run out" of wine.

[57]

HOW TO OPEN YOUR STILL WINE

AS THE OLD ADAGE GOES, to do a job right, you need the right tool. When it comes to opening a bottle of wine, that means using a proper corkscrew. I prefer the ones that many waiters and waitresses use that look like pocketknives versus the ones with the two arms. They have a small blade that is designed to cut through the foil that covers the cork. The perfect place to cut the foil is just below the second lip at the top of the bottle. I've seen many people try to cut the foil at the top lip, but this means that the wine sometimes touches the metal when you pour the wine. It also makes it more difficult to remove the cork.

PRO TIP

Cut the foil below the bottle's second lip to prevent drips.

Use the blade to slice through the foil and then remove it. Then, take the corkscrew and twist it into the cork as deep as you can get it. You can then depress the lever and begin to remove the cork slowly and gently. I also prefer the corkscrews that have two notches on the lever, a long and a short one, that you can use to help you pull the cork out smoothly. Once the cork is out, you can use a cloth or napkin to wipe the glass clean before and after you pour the wine. There are also new technologies available, like electric corkscrews. I personally prefer the old visceral element of powering my own corkscrew.

If you are opening an older bottle of wine, one where the cork might be crumbly, you can use another tool called an **Ah-So**. It's a simple but clever tool where you slide two pieces of metal down into the bottle and around the cork. You then pull the cork out by twisting the metal up and out.

You can also use a **Durand**, which is a combination of both a corkscrew and an Ah-So. It's the ultimate tool for opening wine—but it comes at a hefty price, usually about $200.

Another interesting gadget is called a **Coravin**. This invention, which features a large diameter needle, was designed by a medical equipment maker. It enables you to insert the needle into the cork and extract a sip or a glass of wine without removing the cork. The device also inserts a layer of argon gas that sits on top of the wine to prevent any further oxidation from occurring. You'll see these devices being used in restaurants for their high-end wines by the glass or when sommeliers want to sample a rare wine without fully opening it.

[58]

HOW TO OPEN A BOTTLE OF BUBBLY

SPARKLING WINE OR CHAMPAGNE PAIRS great with food and has that something extra in the bubbles that lets you know it's a party. It's the perfect beverage to celebrate a big event, a marriage, a graduation, or even making it through a tough week. But how do you open a bottle of sparkling wine properly and elegantly?

It's tempting to slide a thumb under the cork and with a triumphant POP, let the cork fly into space. We've all done it, seen it at the end of our favorite NASCAR race or Super Bowl, and it seems like the right thing for a celebration. But a little caution is appropriate. The cork in that Champagne bottle is under a lot of pressure, three times that of the average car tire or around 100 pounds per square inch. The exit velocity has been measured at right around 25 miles per hour!

If it's all the same to you, I'd prefer not to get hit in the eye by any projectile moving that fast, even if it's a cork. To quote Ralphie's mother in *A Christmas Story*, the classic tale of a boy who wanted a BB gun, "You'll shoot your eye out!" At a minimum, you'll ding or damage the ceiling of your host. So how do you open that bottle?

First, you use the knife of your waiter's corkscrew to cut the foil covering and remove it entirely. I have found that the tabs they put in the foil cover are a poor way of removing it. But in a pinch, they will do too.

Second, you remove the cage, which has been placed there for safety. At this point, you are dealing with a loaded weapon, so don't point the cork at anyone as it might pop without notice. Fun fact: The cork cages on all sparkling wines have six turns. Count as you turn—you can impress your friends and win bets with this one.

Third, I like to place a towel or a napkin over the bottle and grip the cork, so it doesn't accidentally open without the cork being under control.

Fourth, with the cork grasped firmly, I slowly turn and rock the bottle to ease the cork out of the bottle. When you get close to pulling the cork, press back into the bottle so the excess CO_2 is released gently. The standard in the wine-serving industry is that it should make the same sound as a nun's fart. In other words, almost no sound at all. If it sounds like a cowboy at a bean supper, you need to move slower when releasing the gas. Trust me, it will impress your friends when you open the bottle without a sound.

PRO TIP

Open your Champagne with as little noise as possible.

Fifth, you place the cork on the table or toss it. Corks for sparkling wine are flared at the bottom and can't be placed back into the bottle if you don't finish it, so they aren't particularly useful after the bottle is open. My simple solution: Make sure you drink the entire bottle!

Sixth, you want to take a small pour and make sure the bottle is good before serving it to your guests. Champagne uses cork and can become corked.

Seventh, pour and enjoy. You shouldn't pour to more than two-thirds of the height of the glass, and I prefer a bit less as a little headspace above the wine helps the experience. It means you are pouring a little more frequently, but it's better than overfilling. Ideally, you should have an ice bucket with a mixture of ice and water available to keep the sparkling wine at the perfect temperature and an arm's length away to refill the glasses of thirsty guests.

If you don't have an ice bucket, toss it in the fridge until you need to refill.

Now, I must admit that I like to pop a cork occasionally like everyone for an auspicious occasion, but the best place to do that is outside and a bit away from a crowd. With a little practice, you will be able to use this more elegant approach for your indoor celebrations involving sparkling wine.

[59]

WHEN DO YOU DECANT A WINE?

ONE OF THE JOBS OF your server or sommelier is to decant the wine, gently pouring a bottle of older wine into an elegant decanter and serving from this fancy glassware, not the bottle. But why do they do this? And when is it appropriate?

There is one main reason to decant a wine and a secondary benefit that you might want to consider. The first is from the technical definition of decant, which is to remove a liquid from a solid precipitate. In the case of red wine, over time, the tannins combine to form longer chain polymers, and while this softens the harsher taste of the wine, it also drops out as a sediment at the bottom of the bottle. Decanting is used to get the wine out while leaving the sediment behind.

Most red wines are filtered before bottling, but some winemakers leave traces of yeast and bits of grapes in the wine, thinking it lends character. These elements will also drop out of the solution over time. Decanting has the same effect on these particles as on the tannin polymers mentioned above.

The second reason to decant a wine is to give it some oxygen exposure and allow the wine to open and release any off-putting flavors. This is particularly useful for wines that are younger and still "tight." An hour or so of air exposure will make them soften and drink as though they are a bit older. You do have to be careful here as the air exposure allows the aromatics to volatilize, and these are the very components that give the wine aroma and flavor—so don't wait too long after decanting to drink up! This is particularly true for ancient red wines, over 20 years old, which are potentially at the end of their drinkable life. An hour in a decanter will close the drinkable window, so you should drink these immediately.

Older red wines, perhaps with 15 to 20 years of age, benefit the most from decanting as they will almost certainly have tannin polymers that can make the drinking experience unpleasant and gritty. No matter the age, if you can see sediment in the bottle, you should decant, so your friends don't get mud in their glass. What is interesting is that younger reds and whites can benefit from the oxygen exposure that allows the wine to open and soften before drinking. When the sommelier asks if I want the wine decanted, I always answer yes. It can't hurt, and it might help!

PRO TIP

Decanting never hurts and probably helps.

When decanting, you should handle the bottle gently, perhaps even leaving it on the side so the sediment doesn't get stirred up and back into the wine. Have your glass pitcher or decanter clean and ready; the size and shape doesn't matter. I've decanted into lovely iced tea pitchers with flowers on the sides as decoration. Gently open the wine, hopefully without disturbing the sediment. Once open, slowly pour the wine into the decanter, looking for the sediment entering the neck of the bottle. Sommeliers will use a candle under the neck to better see the sediment, but I have found the flashlight on my phone to be an excellent option. Once the sediment starts to show, stop pouring. This leaves some wine in the bottle, but the wine in the decanter will be nice and clear.

I have seen some untrained waiters get a lovely decanter, gently open the wine, and then proceed to turn the bottle upside-down and free pour the entire bottle into the glass vessel. This defeats the entire purpose of decanting as the sediment is now nicely mixed into the wine and unlikely to settle out for a few hours.

When to decant? The answer is simple: Old red wines, decant. Younger red and white wines, decant. And when in doubt, decant. It can't hurt.

[60]

GIFTING WINE, SPIRITS, AND WINE ACCESSORIES

IF YOU WANT TO TREAT someone to a bottle of wine, my standard recommendation is to think about getting them something of high quality that they might not otherwise splurge on for themselves. If someone does a big favor for me, for example, I might gift them a bottle that costs $100—something that is special and interesting. A good option in this price range is vintage Champagne. Odds are you can find a bottle that has a vintage they've never enjoyed before.

If you really want to blow their socks off, to reach deep and get something that someone will remember forever, you can explore an auction house to find something special. In cases like these, it can pay to know your audience. For instance, I once bought a $500 bottle from a first-growth producer from an auction for a friend in return for a big favor he did for me. My friend was a wine person, understood the significance of the bottle, and really appreciated the gift. Another great gifting strategy is to get a bottle from a year of significance for the recipient, like when their business opened, when they bought their home, or when their child was born.

The ultimate wine gift, though, if you have enough of a budget, is to gift your own custom-made wine. There are facilities in California that allow you to select the kind of grape for your wine—and then help you design a custom label for it. It can be an amazing way to give a special gift to your customers. But it isn't cheap since you are basically agreeing to buy a barrel of wine—or about 250 bottles of wine. Since each bottle costs between $50 to

$100 depending on your choice of grape, the whole thing could cost between $16,000 and $25,000. Again, this is high-end stuff when it comes to gifting. I have seen this used when giving a gift to the entire firm, like a fancy law firm.

I also have friends who have taken a much more price-conscious approach to gifting bottles of wine. They simply make their own labels and slap them on someone else's wine.

Giving the gift of spirits is another easy option. This is especially true if you grab a bottle of something that you know hits the profile of your friend, like a bourbon or a nice whiskey. Even better if it is a special bottle they might not purchase for themselves. Personally, I love to indulge in the bottle I shared with a friend, to create a memory around the gift as well, if that's an option.

There are plenty of special accessory gifts that you can grab for a business friend that represents how you value the relationship and probably isn't something they would get for themselves. To be fair, these items are mostly wine related, so it is a limited list, but worth considering anyway.

GLASSES

No matter how many glasses one has, a few more never hurts. Some of the better makers include Riedel, Zalto, Schott, and Spiegelau. Now to be fair, these will set you back a few sacks of gold, so you are probably only getting a set of four, unless you really want to wow someone.

The other move on glasses is to go to a basic version of glass and get a dozen for your friend. No one ever has enough wine glasses, so it is usually appreciated.

The final idea is to buy something a bit unusual in a good quality, like Champagne flutes, bourbon glasses, or an American Pinot Noir glass. I must admit, my own collection has a basic set of red wine glasses, white wine glasses, and Champagne flutes.

DECANTER

When I get asked if a wine needs to be decanted, I always answer the same: "Couldn't hurt, might help." Wines almost always benefit from a little air, and it rarely hurts the wine or the experience. But most people have somewhere between one and zero decanters, so it makes a great gift.

There are two ways to go, low and high. A basic decanter can be had on Amazon for between $25 and $50. No need for a stopper either; the whole idea is to get some air into the wine, and I've used a glass pitcher in a pinch, so it really doesn't need to be fancy.

If you want to go high end on a decanter, the sky is the limit for spending. Long-necked elegant glasswork doesn't particularly open the wine to air better than something more basic but the pouring experience from the decanter can be cool. The forms are only limited by the creativity of the glassblower. I try to avoid forms that have skinny, hard-to-clean features, but outside of that, it is a chance for a "wow" gift. But often these items end up collecting dust on a shelf too. We recently bought a $400 decanter for a special client. It was gorgeous, but I sure wouldn't want to have to clean it.

PRO TIP

Don't spring for the fancy cleaning brushes for a decanter.

I just clean mine with a few good swirls of hot water, and I let it drain. You never, ever want to put soap in a decanter or use a brush, even though I know it is tempting to do so.

PRO TIP

Avoid those funky aerators.

They are gimmicky. Between the pour from the bottle, a little time in a decanter, and perhaps a little swirling in the glass, the wine gets plenty of air.

HIGH-END CORKSCREW

A great corkscrew is always a decent gift, and I find myself losing mine all the time—or perhaps leaving them at a friend's home after a bottle or two. Sommeliers swear by their corkscrew, but I like a simple waiter's screw with a double-hinged arm, so I can get two pulls on the cork. This is particularly useful for some European corks, which tend to be longer. Basic versions include HiCoup, OXO, or True. They aren't too expensive, so you could grab a few and stock up your friend or couple it with a bottle of wine (not a screwcap).

If you want to go for artwork that can also be used to open bottles of wine, look to the favorites of high-end sommeliers. A Coutale, Laguiole, or Kershaw are designed to last a lifetime and thousands of bottles of service. They will set you back a few hundred dollars, but they are a great gift for a wine lover. The only issue with these elegant screws is the tears you will shed if they are confiscated at airport security.

PRO TIP

Less is more for corkscrews.

When gifting a corkscrew, don't go for the double-lever version or the single-lever rabbit-style screws, as they can be easy but don't work as well on certain kinds of corks. I also find they offend my minimalist sensibilities—it's a lot of hardware to open a bottle of wine.

For me, the ultimate corkscrew, and one that is specially designed for older corks, is the Durand. It combines a well-made corkscrew with an Ah-Sȯ opener, which is designed to slide two thin pieces of metal along the cork and coax it out without breaking.

I have used mine on some ancient corks and gotten them out without damage.

CORAVIN

A recent development in the wine industry is a device that inserts a high-bore diameter needle from the medical industry through the cork of an unopened bottle and allows you to withdraw a single serving, replacing the wine with inert argon gas. This is a great way to grab a single glass of special wine without opening the whole bottle and having to drink it over the next few days. It's especially good for couples where one does have a glass of wine every so often and the other abstains.

WINE EDUCATION

Who doesn't like to get smarter? Wine education is a phenomenal gift for someone at any stage of their wine life. Not far from my home near Washington, DC is a local wine school that offers classes appropriate for a complete novice up to a national expert. The best part is they do tastings as they educate. Drinking wine and learning is hard to beat, and your friend will always have your gift for them in their head! If you don't know where to start, look for a school that offers classes from Wine and Spirits Education Trust (WSET), an internationally recognized wine program. If there isn't one near you, more excellent schools have moved their content and classes online, so they will come to you.

A WINE BOOK

If you don't want to plunk down the investment for wine education, a wine book is a great alternative. They generally fall into two categories, coffee table books or ones that are more educationally focused. A few of my favorites (besides the book in your hand):

- *The World Atlas of Wine*, by Hugh Johnson

- *Windows on the World Complete Wine Course*, by Kevin Zraly
- *Wine Folly: The Essential Guide to Wine*, by Madeline Puckette and Justin Hammack
- *The Billionaire's Vinegar*, by Benjamin Wallace
- *Cocktail Construction*, by George Watts

And if you don't like any of these, just show up with a bottle of any wine and spend the gift of time with your friend.

[61]

HOW TO CLEAN YOUR WINE GLASSES AND DECANTERS

ANY TIME YOU THROW A dinner party, whether for your boss or some important clients, you want everything to be perfect. But how do you make sure your wine glasses meet the standard? They need to be the right ones, clean, and ready to enjoy wine out of.

Good wine glasses are important to the enjoyment of wine. In part because of that visceral feel of the stem in your hand, but also because great glasses are crafted to feature the aromas of the wine and place the wine on the right part of the tongue. Purchasing good ones can be an investment, as they run from $25 a stem to more than $100 for special ones. Some of the better-known premium brands include names like Reidel and Spiegelau. The good news is that you don't need five sets of glasses: you just need a serviceable set of both red and white wine glasses. My preference is to have about eight of each (some of these will be spares because, trust me, some will get broken). Don't get me wrong, I've had some amazing and memorable wine with friends out of a red Solo cup at a picnic. But dinner parties need stemware.

Let's start from the aftermath of the last dinner party. You're left with dirty glasses, half-drunk glasses, and lipstick on the rims of a few. While it might be tempting to toss them into the dish-washer and head to bed—don't! Stemware needs to be cleaned by hand with lots of hot water and some elbow grease. Soap residue is your enemy when it comes to wine glasses.

The next time you put a wonderful wine into a glass that

contains any of that residue, the soap will go into the wine and make it evil tasting. This is not the way to make an impression at a dinner party. I have had people pour amazing wines into glasses that had some soap residue, and it tasted like soapy dishwater. We all had to pour it out and replace our glasses. You must avoid soap residue at all costs to keep the stemware conditioned for wine.

Ideally, before you head to bed you will carefully handwash the stemware and leave it to dry or even hand-dry it. If you can't muster the energy for that, rinse a few times with water and leave the glasses partially full of water overnight.

The next day, use lots of hot water and rinsing to remove the wine residue. Wine is water-soluble, so this should do the trick. For oil-based stains like lipstick, baking soda and a fine sponge can remove that residue with a little effort. A fully clean glass should sheet water and not spot very much. If you really can't remove a smudge, use the smallest amount of soap you can and rinse very, very completely. You can then leave your glasses to drain in a rack upside down— or better, dry them with a lint-free cloth to remove the water and buff out the water stains.

You should store your glasses bottoms down as you can easily chip the rims of the delicate glasses if you store them top down. This means that some dust will settle in the glasses over time. When you take them out to use, you should use the same lint-free cloth to buff the glasses to remove the dust and any residual water stains. Look through the glass at a light to ensure that the glass is completely clean. You will see sommeliers do this before service in nicer restaurants.

If you use this approach, your guests will arrive to sparkling wine glasses ready to receive a pour of a favorite white or red.

PRO TIP

White wine and salt remove red wine stains.

Accidents happen. What do you do when someone spills some wine? Use white wine to remove a red wine stain. It will dissolve it. Another technique is to use salt. Sprinkle some salt onto the stain, rinse with water, and then blot it out.

CONCLUSION

I SINCERELY HOPE YOU HAVE enjoyed this book. It is the culmination of years of study and decades of entertaining around the world. I have made most of the mistakes in it, and I hope that I have helped you avoid them and handle yourself with confidence in most business settings. Even if you just picked up a few good ideas and some stories to share with friends, I am going to put that in the win column!

If you liked the book, a positive review wherever you bought it and maybe a share on social media would be deeply appreciated.

Cheers!

Jim Schleckser

ACKNOWLEDGMENTS

HENRY SCHLECKSER, MY FATHER, HOOKED me on great wine. I gained much of my knowledge from The Capital Wine School and the Guild of Master Sommeliers. Scott Greenberg has been my wine daddy, and Jim McNair, my wine granddaddy. Rick and John Genderson happily helped me grow my wine cellar. Gene Ford helped grow my love of wine. Master Sommeliers Jarad Slipp, MS, and Andy Meyer, MS, helped educate me. Ellie Benchimol, advanced sommelier, is the leader of my most important tasting group. Thanks to Kennedy Melchiona, Bill Mercurio, Dave Alpher, Sujata Mehta, Raquel Ortega, and Mel Graeff, my tasting buddies.

For helping me create and produce this book, thanks to Darren Dhal, my writing partner; Erin Quinn-Kong, my editor; Lari Bishop, my book wrangler; Sheila Parr, my cover designer; Alex Head, my book designer; David Aretha, my proofreader; Denise Schleckser, my over-enthusiastic proofreader; and Scott Greenberg, my wine editor and proofreader. Sharon McGuire, Pam Singleton, Julie Walker, and Lynn Murphy, my business partners, also contributed.

Also thanks to all the wine professionals and sommeliers who contributed: Ralph Hainsworth, Jefferson Gill Taylor, Brian Williams, Eric E. Ferrell, Josh Copeland, Frank Zarate, Deirdre Lind, Nick Arriagada, Mitchell Scott, Jessica Barger, Ray Maxwell, Justin T. Gavry, Paul Aquino Jr., Nikole Elkins, Winston Duncan, Nikole Elkins, Tân Hùynh, Gaspare Mihalich, David M. Bisenius, Petros Skarmoutsos, Alicia Cuadra-Cutler, Clement Cariot, Gavin Maleson, Jessica Carvalho Carey, Gavin Maleson, Dana Javier, Greg Harrington, and Danny Ippolito.

ABOUT THE AUTHOR

JIM SCHLECKSER IS A CERTIFIED Sommelier from the Court of Master Sommeliers, has an Advanced certification from the Wine and Spirits Education Trust, and is a businessperson with 30 years of professional drinking experience. As the CEO of the Inc. CEO Project, a firm that offers coaching and advising to CEOs of fast-growth companies, he has entertained business associates around the world.

He is committed to helping professionals navigate wine, while keeping it fun. He has a popular blog that speaks to the same topics as this book at ProfessionalDrinking.com, where you can learn more about hiring him as a speaker.

He is an avid soccer player, reader, and outdoorsman.

You can connect with Jim at

ProfessionalDrinking.com

Twitter: @ProDrinking

IncCEOProject.com